Hospitality English for Careers at Hotels

Chiharu Iwai
Ko Masuzaki
Kazunori Nozawa

KINSEIDO

Kinseido Publishing Co., Ltd.
3-21 Kanda Jimbo-cho, Chiyoda-ku,
Tokyo 101-0051, Japan

Copyright © 2015 by Chiharu Iwai
Ko Masuzaki
Kazunori Nozawa

All rights reserved. No part of this publication may be reproduced, stored in a retrieval system, or transmitted, in any form or by any means, electronic, mechanical, photocopying, recording or otherwise, without the prior permission of the publisher.

First published 2015 by Kinseido Publishing Co., Ltd.

Design　　　Nampoosha Co., Ltd.

音声ファイル無料ダウンロード

http://www.kinsei-do.co.jp/download/1142

この教科書で DL 00 の表示がある箇所の音声は、上記 URL または QR コードにて無料でダウンロードできます。自習用音声としてご活用ください。

- ▶ PC からのダウンロードをお勧めします。スマートフォンなどでダウンロードされる場合は、ダウンロード前に「解凍アプリ」をインストールしてください。
- ▶ URL は、検索ボックスではなくアドレスバー（URL 表示覧）に入力してください。
- ▶ お使いのネットワーク環境によっては、ダウンロードできない場合があります。

◎ CD 00 左記の表示がある箇所の音声は、教室用 CD（Class Audio CD）に収録されています。

まえがき

　本書は、ホテルをはじめとする観光業で必要な英語に焦点をあてており、観光業界で働くことを目指す学生、観光業界で現在働いている人、そして、日本の観光業で実際に使える英語を学びたい人に向けて書かれています。

　内容は、大きく分けて、宿泊、レストラン、(観光) 案内、ショップ、そして各部署での苦情対応であり、対面状況だけでなく、電話応対も豊富に取り入れています。全て、実際に起こり得る状況についてニーズ分析した結果に基づいており、具体的かつ実践的な内容になっています。スキットの登場人物は、いわゆる「一流ホテル」のスタッフをモデルとして、ゲストに対し親切丁寧にフレンドリー・サービスを提供しています。さらに、「心を伝えるおもてなし表現」や各Unitの最後に置かれた Useful Tips for Providing Hotel Services では、英語表現や外国人ゲスト応対の際に求められる心構えなどのサービスに関する解説もしています。

　本書は、単にホテルで使える英語を理解し、習得するためだけでなく、日本のゲスト・サービス、すなわち、日本的な「おもてなし」を学び、それを英語で提供するための教材となっています。観光業界で働く人々の活躍を応援する一助となれば幸いです。最後に、本書作成にあたり、ご協力頂きましたホテル業界の皆様と、編集にご尽力頂きました金星堂の皆様に心よりお礼申し上げます。

Unitの構成内容

🛎 Pre-Listening

● **Key Vocabulary**
スキットで使われている重要語彙から出題しています。ここで語彙をしっかり身につけていれば、スキットのリスニングが理解しやすくなります。

● **Understanding Basic Expressions**
外国人ゲストに応対する際に基本的で重要な表現です。発音やイントネーションにも気をつけて正確に覚えましょう。さらに、日本語の意味も考えてみて、日本語と英語の間の表現方法の違いに注意しましょう。

● **心を伝えるおもてなし表現**
Understanding Basic Expressionsやスキットの中から、特に「おもてなし」の精神を伝える温かい表現を中心に紹介しています。また、高度なサービス・スキルに伴う慣用的・機能的な表現などについても解説しています。

🧑‍✈️ While Listening

● **Comprehension Questions A & B**
スキットの流れを確認する問題と、スキットの内容に関する問題です。スキットを正しく理解できているかチェックしましょう。

● **Dictation Exercise**
英文を聞きながら空欄を埋めてスキットを完成させます。細部まで正しく聴き取ることができるか挑戦してみましょう。

🧳 After Listening

● **Writing & Presentation**
各Unitで学習した内容を応用した英作文とプレゼンテーションの課題です。近隣のホテルやレストラン、自分の職場など、身近な状況を使って自由にスキットを考えてみると良いでしょう。

● **Additional Listening & Comprehension Questions**
やや短いスキットのリスニングです。内容が理解できたかどうか、問題を解いてみましょう。最後にスキットの内容を確認し、重要な表現を復習しましょう。

● **Useful Tips for Providing Hotel Services**
Unitのテーマに沿った内容を中心として、ホテルのゲスト・サービスの重要なポイントを様々な角度から紹介しています。プロのサービス・スタッフとしての心構えについても解説しているので、ホテルで仕事をするために必要な基礎的スキルが学べます。また、英語をより効果的に使えるよう、言語的なコミュニケーションだけでなく、表情や態度などの非言語コミュニケーションについても解説しています。

Hospitality English for Careers at Hotels

Contents

Unit 1 1
Room Reservations
Changing a Reservation
宿泊予約／予約変更

Unit 2 7
Checking In at the Front Desk
Giving Directions on the Phone
フロントでのチェック・イン／電話で道案内

Unit 3 13
Checking Out at the Front Desk
Foreign Exchange
フロントでのチェック・アウト／外国通貨両替

Unit 4 19
Showing the Room
Handling a Complaint: Door Lock Problem
客室案内／苦情対応―ドア・ロックの問題

Unit 5 25
Trip to Osaka Castle
Suggesting USJ as a Sightseeing Spot
大阪城観光／USJ観光の提案

Unit 6 31
Lost Articles
Baggage Down
遺失物対応／バゲージ・ダウン

Unit 7 37
Order Taking at a Restaurant: Food Description
Taking an Order for Steak
レストランでのオーダー・テイキング―料理説明／ステーキのオーダー・テイキング

Unit 8 43
Order Taking at a Restaurant: Recommendations
Taking a Breakfast Order
レストランでのオーダー・テイキング―料理提案／朝食のオーダー・テイキング

Unit 9 49
Restaurant Reservations
Handling a Complaint: Misunderstanding Words
レストラン予約／苦情対応―言葉の聞き間違い

Unit 10 55
At the Gift Shop
Handling a Complaint: "No Rolls!"
ギフト・ショップにて／苦情対応―ロールパンがない！

Unit 11 61
Handling a Complaint at the Front Desk: Changing the Room
Bathroom Trouble
フロントでの苦情対応―ルーム・チェンジ／トイレ故障

Unit 12 67
Handling a Complaint at a Restaurant: Order Problems
"Where Is My Lunch?"
レストランでの苦情対応―特別料理注文／私のランチはどこ？

Unit 13 73
Taking Care of a Guest's Illness
Handling a Complaint: No Callback from the Banquet Manager
ゲストが病気になったら？／苦情対応―宴会マネジャーから電話が来ない

Unit 1

Room Reservations
Changing a Reservation

宿泊予約／予約変更

🔔 Pre-Listening

次の定義に当てはまる語句を、選択肢から選びましょう。

[　] 1. a fixed amount of money that is charged or paid for something
[　] 2. an arrangement to secure a place in a hotel or restaurant for future use
[　] 3. occurring before in time or order
[　] 4. the act of asking for something politely or formally
[　] 5. the condition of being able to be used
[　] 6. to feel annoyed about something
[　] 7. to have a great dislike for
[　] 8. to refuse to admit or include
[　] 9. to say that something is true or correct
[　]10. usual, common, or general

| a. availability | b. confirm | c. exclude | d. hate | e. mind |
| f. previous | g. rate | h. reservation | i. request | j. standard |

1

Understanding Basic Expressions

次の基本表現の音声を聞き、どこに強勢（アクセント）を置くか確認しましょう。音声をまねて繰り返し音読し、同時に意味を考えてみましょう。

1. How may I help you?
2. I'd like to make a room reservation.
3. Let me check the availability for you.
4. Thank you for waiting.
5. Would you like a room with twin beds or a double bed?
6. What time will you be arriving?
7. I'm afraid if you'd like your room early in the morning, you need to book the room from the previous night.
8. Would you mind waiting until our check-in time?
9. Let me confirm your reservation now.
10. Thank you very much for your reservation.

心を伝えるおもてなし表現

How may I help you?「いらっしゃいませ」「ご用をお伺いします」
"May I help you?" も同様に使えますが、この how を文頭につけた表現の方が、より積極的にゲストの役に立ちたいという気持ちを表すことができます。

Thank you for waiting.「お待たせいたしました」
英語の表現は「お待ち頂いてありがとうございます」という意味になっています。接客現場でよく使う基本表現です。

May I have the names of the guests, please?
「お泊りのお客様のお名前を伺ってもよろしいでしょうか？」
シンプルに相手の名前を尋ねる時は、"May I have your name?" を使います。"What is your name?" はゲストに使うと失礼になります。

I'm afraid ~「恐れいりますが」「あいにく」
相手の希望に沿えないなど、良くないことを伝えなければいけない時に、言葉を和らげる目的で使います。日本語でも、この和訳の表現はクッション言葉として知られ、接客現場で広く使用されています。

Let me confirm your reservation now.「ご予約を確認させて頂きます」
スキットでは、電話で宿泊予約を受けていますので、復唱して間違いがないか確認しています。

While Listening

Comprehension Questions DL 03, 04   CD 03   CD 04

A 2人の会話を聞き、内容の順に選択肢を並べ替えましょう。

1.____ → 2.____ → 3.____ → 4.____ → 5.____ → 6.____ → 7.____ → 8.____

a. The guest asks the reservationist about the room rate.
b. The guest makes a special request to have a non-smoking room.
c. The guest requests a standard twin-bedded room.
d. The guest says that they will wait until the check-in time.
e. The guest tries to make a reservation by phone for two nights in November.
f. The reservationist checks the room availability.
g. The reservationist confirms the reservation for the guest.
h. The reservationist gives the room rate to the guest.

B 会話の内容に関する質問の答えとして、最も適切な選択肢を選びましょう。

1. How many nights would the guest like to stay at the hotel?
   a. One   b. Two   c. Three   d. Four

2. When are the guests going to arrive at the hotel?
   a. On November 1st   b. On November 21st
   c. On December 1st   d. On December 21st

3. What kind of room type would the guest like to have?
   a. A standard single room   b. A standard double room
   c. A standard twin room   d. A standard triple room

4. How much is the guests' room rate per night?
   a. 13,134 yen   b. 13,340 yen   c. 32,134 yen   d. 32,340 yen

5. When are the guests arriving at the hotel?
   a. Early in the morning   b. Late in the morning
   c. Early in the afternoon   d. Late at night

6. What are the guests going to do with their luggage?

    a. They will take it around.　　**b.** They will leave it at the airport.

    c. They will leave it at the hotel.　　**d.** They will leave it at a JR station.

Dictation Exercise

会話をもう一度聞き、空所に語句を書き入れましょう。

DL 03　CD 03

Guest: Hello.

Reservationist: Hello. This is Reservations, Suzuki speaking. How may I help you?

G: Hello, Ms. Suzuki. I'd like to ¹._____.

R: Thank you very much, sir. What ²._____ are you interested in?

G: Two nights, on November 21st and 22nd.

R: Let me check the ³._____ for you. Just one moment, please.

G: Sure, of course.

R: Thank you for waiting, sir. Yes, we do have some rooms available for those days.

G: How much are your ⁴._____, please?

R: It depends on the ⁵._____ and the number of guests, sir.

G: I'd like a standard room. For two people.

R: Certainly, sir. Would you like a room with twin beds or ⁶._____?

G: I'd like twin beds, please.

R: All right. The room rate for a standard twin-bedded room is ⁷._____ yen per night. The rate excludes tax and a ⁸._____.

G: OK, I'll take that room.

R: Thank you very much, sir. May I have the ⁹._____, please?

G: Sure. It will be me and my wife. Frank and Mary Smith.

DL 04　CD 04

Reservationist: Thank you very much, Mr. Smith. Do you have ¹⁰._____ _____ for your room?

Guest: Oh, I ¹¹._____ the smell of smoke. Do you have a non-smoking room?

R: Certainly, Mr. Smith. I'll reserve a non-smoking room for you.

G: Thank you.

R: You're welcome. 12._____ will you be arriving?

G: Our flight is very early in the morning and so we'll be arriving at about 13._____. Can we check in then?

R: I'm afraid if you'd like your room early in the morning, you need to book the room from the 14._____. So, you'll be charged for one more night. Or, would you mind waiting until our check-in time, 15._____? We can keep your luggage until then.

G: OK, I'll wait then. We'll just 16._____ our luggage.

R: Thank you. Then, let me 17._____ now. That's a reservation of a non-smoking standard twin-bedded room for two nights 18._____ November 21st. The guests' names are Mr. Frank Smith and Mrs. Mary Smith.

G: 19._____. Thank you very much.

R: Thank you very much 20._____.

G: Good-bye.

R: Good-bye, Mr. Smith.

📠 After Listening

Writing & Presentation

ペアを作り、宿泊予約の会話を作ってみましょう。ゲストの名前、滞在日、滞在日数の長さ、客室のタイプ、特別な要望などを自由に変更して考えてみましょう。そして、グループ同士で、あるいはクラス全体でプレゼンテーションしてみましょう。

Additional Listening & Comprehension Questions

2人の会話を聞き、内容に関する質問の答えとして最も適切な選択肢を選びましょう。

🎧 DL 05, 06   💿 CD 05   💿 CD 06

1. What is the purpose of the guest's call?
   a. To complain about the service   b. To thank the reservationist
   c. To change a reservation   d. To make a reservation

2. When is the guest arriving at the hotel?
   a. On August 3rd   b. On August 31st
   c. On October 3rd   d. On October 31st

3. How long does the guest want to extend his stay?
   a. One night   b. Two nights   c. Three nights   d. Four nights

4. What kind of room does the guest have for the third night now?
   a. Suite   b. Standard   c. Deluxe   d. Single

Useful Tips for Providing Hotel Services

Friendly Service とは

欧米の一流ホテルの多くは Friendly Service を謳っています。「フレンドリー」だから、友達のようにゲストに接するサービスという意味ではありません。ゲストに敬意を払いつつも、親しみのある温かいサービスを提供することを意味します。Friendly Service には、サービス提供者としてゲストに関心を持ち、その気持ちを汲んでニーズを察知し、それを言葉や態度で表現して、相手に働きかけることが重要です。日本の社会でも、他者との良い関係を築くためには、積極的に意思疎通を図って理解し合い、相手の気持ちを尊重することが求められます。Friendly Service を提供する際にも同じ心構えでゲストに応対すると良いでしょう。さらに、サービスは言葉とともに、表情や態度も重要です。笑顔も Friendly Service の一つであるため、今回のように電話でゲストに応対する時も笑顔で話します。笑顔で話すと発声やイントネーションが自然に明るく温かいものになり、それがゲストに伝わるからです。本教材の「心を伝えるおもてなし表現」では、Friendly Service をよく表している表現を中心に紹介しています。Understanding Basic Expressions やスキットの音声で、発音やイントネーションを真似しながら、気持ちを込めて言えるようになりましょう。

Unit 2

Checking In at the Front Desk
Giving Directions on the Phone

フロントでのチェック・イン／電話で道案内

Pre-Listening

Key Vocabulary

次の定義に当てはまる語句を、選択肢から選びましょう。

[ ] 1. a small lightweight portable computer
[ ] 2. an area where guests are registered
[ ] 3. suitcases or bags containing personal belongings for a journey
[ ] 4. the act of recording information on an official list
[ ] 5. to complete a document with necessary information
[ ] 6. to expect that something good will happen
[ ] 7. to see a pleasant, distant sight
[ ] 8. to pay all the charges
[ ] 9. to say each letter of a word in order
[ ]10. tools or machines needed for a particular job or activity

| **a.** command a view | **b.** equipment | **c.** fill out | **d.** hope | **e.** laptop |
| **f.** luggage | **g.** reception | **h.** registration | **i.** settle the bill | **j.** spell out |

Understanding Basic Expressions

次の基本表現の音声を聞き、どこに強勢（アクセント）を置くか確認しましょう。音声をまねて繰り返し音読し、同時に意味を考えてみましょう。

1. Could you spell out your last name, please?
2. Could you fill out this registration card for me, please?
3. Will you be staying with us for three nights?
4. How would you like to settle your bill?
5. Here is your room key card.
6. Wi-Fi is available throughout the hotel.
7. We have a fitness center with the latest equipment on the 6th floor.
8. The swimming pool commands a fine view of the city.
9. Our bellboy will help you with your luggage and show you to your room.
10. I hope you will enjoy your stay with us.

 心を伝えるおもてなし表現

Don't worry.「ご心配には及びません」
相手が落胆している時や、心配している時、この表現で強く励ますことができます。イントネーションや顔の表情にも気をつけて、ゲストの不安を払しょくできるように言いましょう。

That's a good idea.「それは良いお考えです」
相手の提案や考えなどを褒める表現です。相手の言うことに強く同意する意味もあります。日本語ではゲストの言うことに「それは良いお考えです」などと言うと失礼になる場合もありますが、英語では褒め言葉です。

Do you have any other questions?「他にご質問はございませんか？」
この表現は、ゲストの質問に積極的に答えようとする姿勢を伝えることができます。ゲストが疑問に思っていることを解消できるよう、この表現を有効に使いましょう。

I hope you will enjoy your stay with us.
「どうか当ホテルでのご宿泊をお楽しみください」
この表現は、これから宿泊するゲストに対して使用します。ホテルでゲストがすばらしい時間を過ごせるように心から願う温かい表現です。日本語では手紙の文末などにこのような願いや祈りの言葉を書きますが、会話では使わないので馴染みが薄いかもしれません。しかし、英語ではよく言いますので、I hope を適切な表現と組み合わせて積極的に使用しましょう。

While Listening

Comprehension Questions   DL 08, 09 CD 08 CD 09

A 2人の会話を聞き、内容の順に選択肢を並べ替えましょう。

1.___ → 2.___ → 3.___ → 4.___ → 5.___ → 6.___ → 7.___ → 8.___

a. The front desk clerk asks the guest about the length of her stay.
b. The front desk clerk asks the guest about the payment method.
c. The front desk clerk asks the guest to complete the registration form.
d. The front desk clerk asks the guest's last name.
e. The front desk clerk explains the gym facilities of the hotel and the hours they are open.
f. The front desk clerk informs the guest of the floor number.
g. The front desk clerk offers to help the guest with her luggage and show her to her room.
h. The guest asks about Internet access.

B 会話の内容に関する質問の答えとして、最も適切な選択肢を選びましょう。

1. What is the guest's family name?
   a. Champ   b. Chapel   c. Campbell   d. Chambull

2. How is the guest going to pay her bill?
   a. In cash   b. With a credit card
   c. With traveler's checks d. With a paycheck

3. What kind of Internet access is available in the room?
   a. Wi-Fi only   b. LAN cable only   c. Wi-Fi and LAN cable   d. Unknown

4. Which floor is the fitness center located on?
   a. B1   b. 5th   c. 6th   d. 7th

5. How many hours are the gym facilities open?
   a. 8 hours   b. 10 hours   c. 12 hours   d. 15 hours

6. What kind of spa is available?
   a. A spa with a whirlpool bath
   b. A spa with a dry sauna
   c. A spa with a mist sauna
   d. A spa with dry and mist saunas

Dictation Exercise

会話をもう一度聞き、空所に語句を書き入れましょう。

DL 08　CD 08

Front Desk Clerk: Good afternoon, ma'am. How may I help you?

Guest: I'd like to ⁱ·_____.

F: Thank you. May I have your last name, please?

G: Campbell.

F: Could you ²·_____ your last name, please?

G: Sure. C-A-M-P-B-E-L-L.

F: Thank you, Ms. Campbell. Could you also ³·_____ this ⁴·_____ card for me, please?

G: OK.

F: Thank you, Ms. Campbell. Will you be ⁵·_____ us for three nights?

G: Yes. That's correct.

F: And how would you like to ⁶·_____, Ms. Campbell?

G: With my credit card.

F: May I have your credit card, ma'am?

G: Sure.

F: Thank you, ma'am. Here's your card back.

DL 09　CD 09

After assigning the guest room.

Front Desk Clerk: Thank you for waiting, Ms. Campbell. Your room is on the ⁷·_____ floor. Here is your room key card.

Guest: Oh, I have a question. I heard I can use the Internet ⁸·_____ _____ in the room. How can I ⁹·_____ the Internet?

F: Wi-Fi is available throughout the hotel. Or you can *10.*_____ to the Internet by using a LAN cable.

G: That's good. Oh, and I want to try the hotel *11.*_____.

F: Well, we have *12.*_____ with the latest equipment on the *13.*_____ floor. We also have a swimming pool and a spa on the *14.*_____ floor. Towels are available at the reception desk. The fitness center and spa are open from 6:30 a.m. to 9:30 p.m. They are *15.*_____ our hotel guests.

G: That's great. Oh, I *16.*_____ my swimsuit.

F: Don't worry, Ms. Campbell. We can lend you a swimsuit at the reception desk of the swimming pool.

G: That's wonderful. I'll go to the gym first, and then I'll go to the swimming pool.

F: That's a good idea, because the swimming pool *17.*_____ a fine view of the city. It has tables and chairs, and you can have drinks, too. Oh, don't forget to enjoy the spa *18.*_____. It is a nice spa with dry and mist saunas.

G: Sure, I will.

F: Do you have any other questions, Ms. Campbell?

G: No, not right now. I'll call you if *19.*_____.

F: Please do. Our bellboy will help you with your *20.*_____ and show you to your room.

G: Thank you.

F: You're welcome, Ms. Campbell. I hope you will enjoy your stay with us.

📋 After Listening

Writing & Presentation

ペアを作り、ゲストがフロント・スタッフに喫煙ルームから禁煙ルームへ変更を依頼する会話を作ってみましょう。ゲストの名前、希望する部屋の種類、宿泊人数、特別な要望などを自由に変更して考えてみましょう。希望通り禁煙ルームに変更できる場合だけでなく、喫煙ルームしか他に空室がない場合も想定し、他の条件でゲストを納得させられる提案をしてみましょう。そして、グループ同士で、あるいはクラス全体でプレゼンテーションしてみましょう。

Additional Listening & Comprehension Questions

2人の会話を聞き、内容に関する質問の答えとして最も適切な選択肢を選びましょう。

🎧 DL 10, 11　　💿 CD 10　　💿 CD 11

1. How many nights does the guest plan to stay at the hotel?

    a. One　　**b**. Two　　**c**. Three　　**d**. Four

2. Where is the guest now?

    a. At an airport　　**b**. In a station　　**c**. On a bus　　**d**. At home

3. What's the problem with the guest?

    a. He has lost the map to the airport.　　**b**. He has heavy luggage with him.

    c. He has missed his bus.　　**d**. He has no problems.

4. Where does the airport limousine leave from?

    a. From the 1st floor of Terminal 1　　**b**. From the 2nd floor of Terminal 1

    c. From the 1st floor of Terminal 2　　**d**. From the 2nd floor of Terminal 2

Useful Tips for Providing Hotel Services

設備やサービスをアピールする

フロントはホテルの顔と言われます。フロントはどこのホテルにもあり、宿泊するゲストが必ず訪れる場所で、ありとあらゆる問い合わせがあります。従って、フロント・スタッフは宿泊に関する専門のオペレーションを適切に行うだけでなく、ホテルの全ての施設やサービスについての知識を持ち、それを必要としているゲストに提供しなければなりません。今回のスキットでは、フロント・スタッフはホテルのジム（フィットネス・センターなどの屋内トレーニング室）の設備とサービスを詳細に説明するとともに、その素晴らしさをゲストにアピールしています。説明することだけに意識を集中せず、これから利用しようとしているゲストの立場に立って、その良さを生き生きと表現すれば、コミュニケーションに温かさが生まれます。そして、ゲストに利用して頂き、喜んで頂けるとホテル全体の印象も良くなり、顧客満足度を高めることに繋がるのです。

Checking Out at the Front Desk
Foreign Exchange

フロントでのチェック・アウト／外国通貨両替

🛎 Pre-Listening

次の定義に当てはまる語句を、選択肢から選びましょう。

[　] 1. an outer garment, such as a cape or a coat
[　] 2. a small semi-enclosed room
[　] 3. a sum
[　] 4. hindrance, trouble, or difficulty
[　] 5. the handwritten name of a person
[　] 6. the small refrigerator holding drinks and snacks in a hotel room
[　] 7. to make some liquid flow out of something
[　] 8. to pay the bill and depart from a hotel
[　] 9. to reach a sum of money or to total
[　]10. to willingly take something that someone offers you

| **a.** accept | **b.** amount | **c.** check out | **d.** cloak | **e.** come to |
| **f.** drain | **g.** inconvenience | **h.** minibar | **i.** signature | **j.** stall |

Understanding Basic Expressions

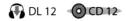

次の基本表現の音声を聞き、どこに強勢（アクセント）を置くか確認しましょう。音声をまねて繰り返し音読し、同時に意味を考えてみましょう。

1. Did you have anything from the minibar last night or this morning?
2. How was your stay with us?
3. We're terribly sorry for the inconvenience.
4. The total comes to 75,342 yen.
5. How would you like to pay?
6. Here you are.
7. Is there anything valuable or breakable in this bag?
8. I'm afraid we can't accept any items that are valuable or breakable.
9. It is against our hotel policy.
10. I have to say we can't keep them in the cloak room.

心を伝えるおもてなし表現

How was your stay with us?「ご宿泊はいかがでしたか？」
出発するゲストに対し、宿泊の感想を聞くことは非常に重要なサービスです（詳しくは、P. 18 の Useful Tips for Providing Hotel Services を参照）。気持ちを込めて上手に言えるように、何度も練習しておきましょう。

We're terribly sorry for the inconvenience.「ご不便をおかけして大変申し訳ございません」
inconvenience は不便、不快、不自由などを示し、トラブルに対して広く使えます。

Of course, sir.「(sirは男性、ma'amは女性ゲストに対して)もちろんでございます」
この表現は、ゲストの依頼や問い合わせへの強い同意、承諾を意味します。日本語でもこの表現（「もちろんでございます」）を効果的に使用する接客場面が多く見られます。

I have to say we can't keep them in the cloak room.
「残念ながら、クロークルームではこれらのお荷物をお預かりすることはできません」
I have to say は（ゲストの希望には沿いたいが、その）自分の意に反して言わなければならないということを意味し、とても丁寧な表現になります。

Thank you so much for your understanding.「ご理解頂き、誠にありがとうございます」
こちらの事情を説明して、ゲストにご納得頂いた時に、この表現で協力して頂いた感謝の気持ちを伝えます。

Have a nice day!「良い一日をお過ごしください」
ゲストとの別れ際に必ず言うと良いでしょう。夕方が近くなってきたら、"Have a nice evening!" という表現になります。さらに、ゲストが帰国することを知っている場合は、"Have a nice trip back home!" と言うこともできます。

While Listening

Comprehension Questions 🎧 DL 13, 14 💿 CD 13 💿 CD 14

A 2人の会話を聞き、内容の順に選択肢を並べ替えましょう。

1.____ → 2.____ → 3.____ → 4.____ → 5.____ → 6.____ → 7.____ → 8.____

a. The front desk clerk apologizes to the guest for the inconvenience of the shower.
b. The front desk clerk asks the guest his room number.
c. The front desk clerk shows the guest the bill.
d. The guest complains about the shower stall which didn't drain well.
e. The guest says that he wants to leave his bag at the hotel.
f. The guest takes out the watch and the bottles of sake from his bag.
g. The guest tells the front desk clerk that he did not use the minibar.
h. The guest tells the front desk clerk when he will be back.

B 会話の内容に関する質問の答えとして、最も適切な選択肢を選びましょう。

1. What was wrong with the guest's room?
   a. The minibar   b. The shower stall   c. The TV   d. The toilet

2. How does the guest feel about the problem he had in his room?
   a. Angry   b. OK   c. Sad   d. Glad

3. What does the guest need to do after checking the bill?
   a. Pay the bill in cash   b. Pay the bill with his credit card
   c. Complain about the total amount   d. Give the front desk clerk the receipt

4. Why does the guest want to leave the bottles of sake at the hotel?
   a. Because he will not use them anymore.
   b. Because they are broken and useless.
   c. Because they are heavy and he does not want to carry them around.
   d. Because they will be picked up by his friend later.

5. Based on the hotel policy, which of the following items can the hotel accept when guests leave their bags?
   a. Cash   b. Credit cards   c. Jewelry   d. Books

6. How does the guest react when he is informed of the hotel policy?

    a. He makes a complaint about it.   **b.** He rejects it.

    c. He misunderstands it.   **d.** He follows it.

Dictation Exercise

会話をもう一度聞き、空所に語句を書き入れましょう。

🎧 DL 13   💿 CD 13

Front Desk Clerk: Good morning, sir.

Guest: Good morning. I'm ^{1.}_____.

F: May I have your room number, please?

G: Yes. It's ^{2.}_____.

F: Thank you, Mr. Taylor. Did you have anything from the ^{3.}_____ last night or this morning?

G: No, I didn't.

F: Thank you, Mr. Taylor. How was your stay with us?

G: I enjoyed it very much, but the water in the ^{4.}_____ doesn't ^{5.}_____. It was not a big problem for me, but I think you should check it later.

F: We're terribly sorry ^{6.}_____. I'll ask the maintenance department to ^{7.}_____. Thank you for that information.

G: You're welcome.

F: Here is your ^{8.}_____, Mr. Taylor. The total ^{9.}_____ 75,342 yen. Could you check each item and the total amount, please?

G: OK. This is fine.

F: How would you like to pay?

G: I'll pay by credit card. Here you are.

F: Thank you. May I just ^{10.}_____ here, please?

G: Sure.

F: Thank you, Mr. Taylor. Here is ^{11.}_____.

Guest: Thank you. By the way, can I leave this bag with you?

Front Desk Clerk: Of course, sir. Is there anything valuable or breakable in it?

G: Ah, yes. It has ⁱ². _____ sake and a new watch.

F: I'm afraid we can't accept ¹³. _____ that are valuable or breakable, sir. Could you please carry them with you?

G: OK. Then, I'll ¹⁴. _____ the watch. But the bottles of sake . . . they're very heavy and ¹⁵. _____. I don't mind if they are broken. So can you keep them for me?

F: I'm really sorry about this. But it is against ¹⁶. _____ _____. I have to say we can't keep them in the ¹⁷. _____.

G: OK. I'll carry them, too.

F: Thank you so much for your understanding. We'll keep this bag for you. What time will you be back?

G: I'll come back at ¹⁸. _____.

F: Very well, Mr. Taylor. This is the ¹⁹. _____.

G: Thank you.

F: You're welcome. Have a nice day!

G: Thank you. ²⁰. _____.

After Listening

Writing & Presentation

ペアを作り、ミニバーで飲み物（ソフトドリンク、アルコール類）を飲んだり、食べ物（ナッツ、クッキー、クラッカー等）を食べたことを前提にしたゲストとフロント・スタッフの会話や、支払方法をクレジットカードではなく、現金のみで、あるいは現金とクレジットカードの組み合わせなどに変更する会話を作ってみましょう。飲み物や食べ物の種類と利用した数、支払方法の組み合わせなどを自由に変更して考えてみましょう。スタッフはできるだけゲストの希望に沿うよう丁寧に教えてあげましょう。そして、グループ同士で、あるいはクラス全体でプレゼンテーションしてみましょう。

Additional Listening & Comprehension Questions

2人の会話を聞き、内容に関する質問の答えとして最も適切な選択肢を選びましょう。

 DL 15, 16   CD 15   CD 16

1. What does the guest want to exchange?

    a. Yen into US dollars   b. US dollars into yen   c. Her room   d. Her ID

2. What does the front desk clerk want to know?

    a. The guest's problem   b. The guest's room number
    c. Today's exchange rate   d. Today's economic news

3. How much yen does the guest receive if she exchanges one dollar?

    a. 95 yen   b. 100 yen   c. 105 yen   d. 110 yen

4. What does the guest do just before finishing the exchange?

    a. Give her name   b. Show her passport
    c. Sign her name   d. Give her room number

Useful Tips for Providing Hotel Services

宿泊の感想を聞く

Unit 3 のスキットでは、チェック・アウトの際に、フロント・スタッフがゲストに "How was your stay with us?" と尋ねています。もし、ゲストが滞在中であれば、was を現在形にして "How is your stay with us?" と尋ねます。ゲストに感想を聞くことは重要なサービスの一つであり、ゲストが満足しているかどうかを気遣う気持ちを伝えることができます。また、もし何か問題があればそれを言う機会をゲストに提供でき、その問題に迅速で的確な対処をすればゲストの不満を最小限に抑え、満足度を高めることも可能なのです。さらに、ゲストの感想や意見はホテルにとって貴重な情報であり、サービスの向上やホテルの社員教育にも活用されます（レストランでも感想を聞くサービスがあります。詳しくは、Unit 8 の Useful Tips for Providing Hotel Services を参照）。

Unit 4

Showing the Room
Handling a Complaint: Door Lock Problem

客室案内／苦情対応―ドア・ロックの問題

🔔 Pre-Listening

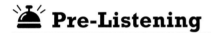

次の定義に当てはまる語句を、選択肢から選びましょう。

[   ] 1. a hallway connecting parts of a building
[   ] 2. a meal at which guests serve themselves
[   ] 3. a metal container with a secure lock for storing valuables
[   ] 4. a number of different types of things
[   ] 5. a place or a piece of equipment designed for a particular purpose
[   ] 6. a sudden occurrence of some danger which needs immediate action
[   ] 7. the act of giving a small sum of money to a porter or restaurant server for their services
[   ] 8. to describe something clearly to make it understandable
[   ] 9. to set something in its proper place for use
[   ] 10. useful for someone's needs

a. buffet	**b.** convenient	**c.** corridor	**d.** emergency	**e.** explain
f. facility	**g.** install	**h.** safe	**i.** tipping	**j.** variety

Understanding Basic Expressions

次の基本表現の音声を聞き、どこに強勢（アクセント）を置くか確認しましょう。音声をまねて繰り返し音読し、同時に意味を考えてみましょう。

1. I'll show you to your room.
2. Here we are.
3. After you.
4. The emergency exit is at the end of the corridor.
5. Would you like me to show you the room facilities?
6. Room service is available 24 hours a day.
7. Is there anything else I can do for you?
8. Would you like a Japanese style or a Western style breakfast?
9. That's very kind of you.
10. We don't accept tips in this hotel.

 心を伝えるおもてなし表現

After you.「お先にどうぞ」
ゲストに先に行って頂く時に使います。英語では、「（私は）あなたの後に」という意味になっています。

The emergency exit is at the end of the corridor.
「非常口は廊下の突き当たりにございます」
宿泊されるゲストの安全を守るため、非常口の案内をすることは必須の業務です。

Would you like me to show you the room facilities?
「客室内の設備をご説明いたしましょうか？」
スキットのベルボーイのように、この表現でゲストの意向を確認してから客室内の設備の説明をする方が丁寧で良いでしょう。

Is there anything else I can do for you?「他にご用はございませんか？」
一通り用事が終わったら、他にできることがないかをこの表現で尋ねてみましょう。また、この文の中でfor youという表現が英語らしく、文字通り「あなたのために」ということを表現します。日本語では敢えて言わないことですが、for youを積極的に使って、おもてなしの心を伝えましょう。

That's very kind of you.「それはご親切にありがとうございます」
本スキットでは、チップの受け取りを断る場面でこの表現を使っています。この場合、"No." だけではあまりにも失礼ですので、この表現で相手の心遣いを認識し、感謝していることを表現しましょう。これは、断りの場面だけでなく、感謝する場面でも使えます。

While Listening

Comprehension Questions DL 18, 19 CD 18 CD 19

A 2人の会話を聞き、内容の順に選択肢を並べ替えましょう。

1.____ → 2.____ → 3.____ → 4.____ → 5.____ → 6.____ → 7.____ → 8.____

a. The bellboy and the guest approach the elevator.
b. The bellboy and the guest go up to the 15th floor.
c. The bellboy asks if the guest wants him to explain the room facilities.
d. The bellboy gives the guest a room key card.
e. The bellboy politely refuses the tip.
f. The bellboy shows the guest the emergency exit.
g. The guest asks the bellboy where she can have breakfast.
h. The guest tries to give the bellboy a tip.

B 会話の内容に関する質問の答えとして、最も適切な選択肢を選びましょう。

1. What explains many of the hotel's services?
   a. The hotel information book   b. The room key card
   c. Wi-Fi service   d. TV programs

2. What is in the night table?
   a. The hotel information book   b. The room safe
   c. A LAN cable   d. The air-conditioner control

3. What can the guest do while she is taking a bath?
   a. Watch TV   b. Make a phone call
   c. Watch DVDs   d. Have Internet access

4. What is the Lounge Cafe?
   a. A buffet-style restaurant
   b. A restaurant with traditional Japanese dishes
   c. A self-service restaurant
   d. A restaurant with a wide variety of dishes

5. Why does the bellboy refuse the tip from the guest?
    a. Because he is very kind.
    b. Because he has already got enough tips.
    c. Because they don't accept tips in the hotel.
    d. Because the hotel has a tipping system.

Dictation Exercise

会話をもう一度聞き、空所に語句を書き入れましょう。

DL 18　CD 18

Bellboy: I'll show you to your room, ma'am. May I ^{1.}_____?

Guest: Yes, please.

B: Follow me, please. Your elevator is this way.

G: I see.

B: ^{2.}_____. We'll take this elevator up to the 15th floor. After you, Ms. Scott.

G: Thank you.

B: This is the 15th floor. Your room is ^{3.}_____, Ms. Scott. The ^{4.}_____ is at the end of the ^{5.}_____. Here is your room, ^{6.}_____. After you, please. May I ^{7.}_____ here?

G: Sure.

B: Here is your room key card.

G: Thank you.

B: Would you like me to show you the ^{8.}_____?

G: Yes, I would.

B: The ^{9.}_____ is here on the wall. And the hotel information book on this table explains many of the hotel's services. ^{10.}_____ is available, but we also have this ^{11.}_____ for Internet access. Room service is available ^{12.}_____. The ^{13.}_____ is very convenient and it's in the night table. I'll show you the bathroom. You can watch TV or listen to the radio ^{14.}_____

22

on the wall while taking a bath in this nice, comfortable bathtub. And there is also a separate shower stall. Is there ^{15.}_____ I can do for you, Ms. Scott?

🎧 DL 19   💿 CD 19

Guest: Well . . . oh, I have a question. Where can I have breakfast tomorrow morning?

Bellboy: Would you like a Japanese style or a Western style breakfast?

G: I'd like Western.

B: I see. For breakfast, there are two restaurants in the hotel. One is the Lounge Cafe on the 1st floor. It is a big restaurant where you can enjoy ^{16.}_____ _____ dishes. And the other is a ^{17.}_____ restaurant called Akari. It is an ^{18.}_____ restaurant and it's on the 5th floor.

G: OK. Then I'll try Restaurant Akari tomorrow. Thank you.

B: You're quite welcome, Ms. Scott.

G: Here is ^{19.}_____.

B: That's very kind of you, ma'am. But we don't ^{20.}_____ in this hotel.

G: Well, thank you very much.

B: Please enjoy your stay.

🧳 After Listening

Writing & Presentation

ペアを作り、客室案内係（ベルボーイ）が提供する情報（ゲストの客室のある階数、エレベータを降りてからの部屋に向かう方向、利用できるインターネット接続の方法、朝食を取るレストランの名称や料理の種類など）を適宜変更して会話を作ってみましょう。そして、グループ同士で、あるいはクラス全体でプレゼンテーションしてみましょう。

Additional Listening & Comprehension Questions

2人の会話を聞き、内容に関する質問の答えとして最も適切な選択肢を選びましょう。

1. What's the guest's problem?
   a. The room door doesn't lock.　　b. He doesn't like the front desk clerk.
   c. He doesn't know the room number.　　d. He can't enjoy rock music.

2. Which room is the guest staying in?
   a. 1517　　b. 1715　　c. 1750　　d. 1550

3. When will the front desk clerk visit the guest's room?
   a. In the evening　　b. Later　　c. Soon　　d. Never

4. When will the technician visit the guest's room?
   a. In the evening　　b. Later　　c. Soon　　d. Never

Useful Tips for Providing Hotel Services

ゲストとの会話の機会が多いベル・サービス

ベル・サービスはホテル内や客室を案内中にゲストと長い時間をともにするため、ゲストと話をする機会が多いものです。その間、ゲストにとっていかに有益で楽しい時間にできるかが腕の見せ所です。まず、ゲストの名前を把握したら、できる限り Mr. ～、M(r)s. ～と言って名前でゲストに呼びかけましょう。できれば、そのゲストが出発するまで名前を覚えておき接客の際に常に言えると良いでしょう。また、話をする時は、ゲストの目を見て話すことが大切です。日本人は shy な人が多いですが、目を見て話をしなければ、英語圏の人には不誠実と受け取られる恐れがあります。正しい英語を覚えていてもそれだけでは真心が通じませんから、恥ずかしがらず優しいまなざしでしっかりゲストの目を見て話しましょう。ゲストと話をする際の話題としては、ゲストのニーズにあったホテルの施設やサービスの案内、近隣の観光地の紹介などが代表的なものです。個人的な経験などもふまえ、自分の言葉で説明できると、ゲストは興味を持ち喜ばれます。会話が弾めば、スタッフとしても嬉しいものです。

Unit 5

Trip to Osaka Castle
Suggesting USJ as a Sightseeing Spot

大阪城観光／USJ 観光の提案

 **Pre-Listening**

Key Vocabulary

次の定義に当てはまる語句を、選択肢から選びましょう。

[   ] 1. a deep water-filled ditch around a castle for protection against invasion
[   ] 2. aquatic plants
[   ] 3. flowers of a fruit-bearing plant
[   ] 4. the act of entering
[   ] 5. the act of visiting places and things of interest
[   ] 6. the price for taking a bus, train, or airplane
[   ] 7. to be present on all sides of something
[   ] 8. the feeling of something
[   ] 9. to increase the length or duration of something
[   ]10. to spend money or time uselessly

a. admission	**b.** blossoms	**c.** extend	**d.** fare	**e.** moat
f. sense	**g.** sightseeing	**h.** surround	**i.** waste	**j.** waterweed

Understanding Basic Expressions

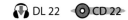

次の基本表現の音声を聞き、どこに強勢（アクセント）を置くか確認しましょう。音声をまねて繰り返し音読し、同時に意味を考えてみましょう。

1. How about visiting Osaka Castle?
2. This castle is one of the most popular spots for international tourists.
3. You need no reservation.
4. The castle tower is open from 9:00 a.m. to 5:00 p.m. daily.
5. The admission fee is 600 yen for adults and free for children up to 15 years old.
6. Can you tell me how to get there?
7. It's only a 10-minute ride.
8. The train fare is 160 yen.
9. It's a 15-minute walk from Osakajo-Koen Station to Osaka Castle.
10. I hope you will like it.

心を伝えるおもてなし表現

How about visiting Osaka Castle?「大阪城に行かれるというのはいかがでしょう？」
"How about ~ ?" で勧める表現です。How about の後、動詞の ing 形を続けます。どこに行ったら良いかアイデアが浮かばないというゲストに対して、この表現で観光スポットの提案をしています。外国からのゲストが興味を持ちそうな観光スポットの情報をあらかじめ用意しておき、ゲストのニーズに合わせて適切に提案できることが重要です。スキットでは、この表現の後で、観光スポットに関連する情報を豊富に提供し、ゲストに喜んで頂いている場面となっています。

I hope you will like it.「お気に召して頂けるとよろしいのですが」
Unit 2 でも紹介した I hope でゲストの幸せを願う表現です。このように、様々な状況で使用できますので、適切な表現と組み合わせて積極的に使用しましょう。

While Listening

Comprehension Questions DL 23, 24   CD 23   CD 24

A 2人の会話を聞き、内容の順に選択肢を並べ替えましょう。

1.____ → 2.____ → 3.____ → 4.____ → 5.____ → 6.____ → 7.____ → 8.____

a. The concierge explains what time the castle tower closes.
b. The concierge recommends that the guest take the JR Loop Line.
c. The concierge suggests a visit to Osaka Castle.
d. The concierge mentions the admission fee for the castle tower.
e. The concierge tells the guest what surrounds the castle.
f. The guest makes the decision to visit Osaka Castle.
g. The guest says that he needs to go to a department store.
h. The guest thinks his son will enjoy the visit to Osaka Castle.

B 会話の内容に関する質問の答えとして、最も適切な選択肢を選びましょう。

1. Which season is it now?
    a. Spring   b. Summer   c. Autumn   d. Winter
2. What time does the castle tower usually open?
    a. At 9:00 a.m.   b. At 9:00 p.m.   c. At 5:00 a.m.   d. At 5:00 p.m.
3. By what time does the concierge advise the guest to enter the castle tower?
    a. 7:00 p.m.   b. 7:30 p.m.   c. 6:00 p.m.   d. 6:30 p.m.
4. How much do children up to 15 years old pay to go up to the top of the castle?
    a. 600 yen   b. 300 yen   c. As much as they like   d. Nothing
5. What is the guest's son interested in?
    a. Japan   b. Castles   c. History   d. Parks
6. Where will the guest go in the morning before visiting Osaka Castle?
    a. Osaka Station   b. Osakajo-Koen Station
    c. A beautiful park   d. A department store

7. How long does it take from Osakajo-Koen Station to Osaka Castle?

   a. 15 minutes by bus
   b. 15 minutes on foot
   c. 10 minutes by bus
   d. 10 minutes on foot

Dictation Exercise

会話をもう一度聞き、空所に語句を書き入れましょう。

DL 23　CD 23

Guest: Good morning.

Concierge: Good morning, sir. How may I help you?

G: I wonder if you could give me some advice on ¹._____ in Osaka. I'm with my son. What should we do today? I don't want to ²._____ this beautiful weather.

C: How about visiting Osaka Castle? This castle is one of ³._____ spots for ⁴._____. It is big and beautiful. I'm sure you can get a ⁵._____ of the history of Osaka just by ⁶._____ the castle.

G: Osaka Castle?

C: The castle ⁷._____ a beautiful park. The park is filled with nature: trees, flowers, ⁸._____, and so on. Now in spring, you can enjoy the ⁹._____ of hundreds of cherry trees. You can also go up to the top of the castle. You need ¹⁰._____, sir.

G: That sounds good.

DL 24　CD 24

Concierge: Just for your information, the castle tower is open from 9:00 a.m. to 5:00 p.m. daily. But now it's the special cherry blossom season, and the closing time ¹¹._____ 7:00 p.m. ¹²._____ enter the tower by 6:30 p.m. The ¹³._____ is 600 yen for adults and free for children ¹⁴._____ years old.

Guest: That sounds nice. My son is also interested in history—especially Japanese history. We'll try the castle today. But I need to go to [15.]_____ _____ near Osaka Station in the morning. So, I'll go to Osaka Castle in the afternoon. Can you tell me how to get there?

C: Of course, sir. Take the JR Loop Line from Osaka Station to Osakajo-Koen Station, [16.]_____. It's only a 10-minute ride. The [17.]_____ _____ is 160 yen.

G: OK.

C: It's [18.]_____ from Osakajo-Koen Station to Osaka Castle.

G: Thank you for your [19.]_____. It'll be pretty nice to [20.]_____ the park and enjoy Japanese history and culture.

C: I hope you'll like it. Have a nice day.

After Listening

Writing & Presentation

ペアを作り、ゲストに楽しく良い思い出となる観光を勧めるため、大阪城以外の場所（たとえば、京都の神社仏閣、東京ディズニーリゾート、浅草、東京スカイツリーなどや、近隣のよく知られている観光スポット）に対応する会話を作ってみましょう。それらの観光地へ行くための交通手段、費用、移動時間などを自由に変更して考えてみましょう。ゲストの希望に沿うように的確なアドバイスをしましょう。そして、グループ同士で、あるいはクラス全体でプレゼンテーションしてみましょう。

Additional Listening & Comprehension Questions

2人の会話を聞き、内容に関する質問の答えとして最も適切な選択肢を選びましょう。

DL 25, 26

1. With whom is the guest going sightseeing?

   a. Her husband   b. Her friend   c. Her son   d. Her daughter

2. How many Universal Studio theme parks were there in the world before Universal Studios Japan was built?

   a. One   b. Two   c. Three   d. Four

3. What decision does the guest make about sightseeing?

   a. To go out to see a movie   b. To walk around
   c. To visit Universal Studios Japan   d. To stay in the hotel

4. According to the concierge, how should the guest go to JR Osaka Station?

   a. On foot   b. By taxi   c. By the hotel's shuttle bus   d. By train

---

Useful Tips for Providing Hotel Services

よろず相談係のコンシェルジュ

Unit 5 では、コンシェルジュがゲストの観光の相談に乗っている場面を紹介しています。コンシェルジュは「よろず相談係」という別名があるように、ゲストのさまざまな相談に対応することが仕事です。スキットのような観光案内や、レストランの予約、各種チケットの手配などをはじめ、ゲストのありとあらゆる相談に乗るため、ホテル業務だけでなく、高度な語学力と異文化理解についての深い知識が必要です。今回の観光案内では、どこに行くべきかについて観光スポットの提案を行っていますが、コンシェルジュ・デスクでは近隣の観光地についての詳細な情報を備えています。また、時にはゲストにメモを書いたり、関連するパンフレットや地図があれば提供したりして、ゲストに理解しやすく、実際に行く時に便利になるような工夫もします。このようにゲストの困りごとを解決するコンシェルジュは、ゲストの強力な助っ人なのです。

Unit 6

Lost Articles
Baggage Down

遺失物対応／バゲージ・ダウン

🔔 Pre-Listening

Key Vocabulary

次の定義に当てはまる語句を、選択肢から選びましょう。

[ ] 1. ahead of time
[ ] 2. an arrangement of keeping money at a bank
[ ] 3. an order for the payment of money issued by a bank or post office
[ ] 4. something inscribed or engraved, as on a watch
[ ] 5. the charge for sending a piece of mail
[ ] 6. to be grateful for
[ ] 7. to check again
[ ] 8. to remain on a telephone line and wait for the other party
[ ] 9. to say or write something again
[ ]10. to tell or write in words

| **a.** account | **b.** appreciate | **c.** describe | **d.** double check | **e.** hold |
| **f.** in advance | **g.** inscription | **h.** money order | **i.** postage | **j.** repeat |

Understanding Basic Expressions

次の基本表現の音声を聞き、どこに強勢（アクセント）を置くか確認しましょう。音声をまねて繰り返し音読し、同時に意味を考えてみましょう。

1. I left my watch in room 1925.
2. Let me check for you.
3. Would you hold the line, please?
4. Could you describe your watch?
5. Let me double check.
6. Would you mind paying the postage in advance?
7. We'll send you an e-mail to tell you the amount of postage.
8. Let me repeat your e-mail address.
9. I really appreciate your help.
10. It's my pleasure.

心を伝えるおもてなし表現

Let me check for you. 「お調べいたします」
この表現では、Unit 4 でも登場した for you を最後につけて「あなたのために」ということを強調しています。これで、調べている間、ゲストに気持ちよく待って頂くことも可能です。

Let me double check. 「もう一度確認します」
前出の "Let me check for you." と言ってからもう一度調べる場合に使います。これは、正確な仕事をしようとしていることも伝えられる表現です。

It's my pleasure. 「それ（ゲストのお役に立つこと）は私の喜びです」
ゲストに感謝された時に接客担当者としての喜びを表す、非常に丁寧な表現です。"It's my great pleasure." という文で「大きな喜びです」と、さらに嬉しい気持ちを表現することもあります。ゲストの "Thank you." に対しては "You're welcome." ももちろん良いですが、特に大きな手助けをしてそれを喜んで頂いた時などにこの表現を使うとよりふさわしいでしょう。

While Listening

Comprehension Questions DL 28, 29 CD 28 CD 29

A 2人の会話を聞き、内容の順に選択肢を並べ替えましょう。

1.____ → 2.____ → 3.____ → 4.____ → 5.____ → 6.____ → 7.____ → 8.____

a. The bellboy explains that the postage should be paid by the woman.
b. The woman asks the bellboy how she should pay the postage.
c. The woman asks the bellboy to send the watch to her.
d. The woman chooses the method of payment most convenient for her.
e. The woman describes the brand and the color of her watch.
f. The woman gives the bellboy her e-mail address.
g. The woman tells the bellboy about the inscription on her watch.
h. The woman tells the bellboy that she left one of her belongings in the hotel.

B 会話の内容に関する質問の答えとして、最も適切な選択肢を選びましょう。

1. Who is the woman that calls the Bell Service?
   a. A hotel resident
   b. A Bell Service staff member
   c. A businessperson who worked for a bank
   d. A person who stayed at the hotel

2. What is wrong with the woman?
   a. Her watch is missing.   b. Her watch is broken.
   c. She cannot watch TV.   d. She cannot pay the postage.

3. What does the woman talk about?
   a. A children's watch   b. A men's watch
   c. A silver watch   d. David's watch

4. Where does the woman live?
   a. In Japan   b. In Chicago   c. In California   d. Unknown

5. What payment option does the woman take?
   a. Paying by credit card
   b. Paying by cash
   c. Paying into the hotel's bank account
   d. Paying by international postal money order

6. What is her e-mail address?
   a. maryclark@abcd.com
   b. Maryclark@abcd.com
   c. mary-clark@abcd.com
   d. mary_clark@abcd.com

Dictation Exercise

会話をもう一度聞き、空所に語句を書き入れましょう。

DL 28　CD 28

Bellboy: Good afternoon, this is the ^{1.}_____, Matsukawa speaking. How may I help you?

Guest: I think I left my watch in room ^{2.}_____ when I stayed there on ^{3.}_____.

B: All right, ma'am. Let me check for you. Would you ^{4.}_____, please?

G: Sure, of course.

B: Thank you for waiting. We have two watches that were left in ^{5.}_____ _____. Could you describe your watch?

G: My watch is a Cartier, ^{6.}_____.

B: What color is it, ma'am?

G: It's ^{7.}_____.

B: OK. Let me ^{8.}_____. . . . We do have a Cartier watch. Is there any ^{9.}_____?

G: Sure. It says "With All My Heart, David. Nov. 19, 1998."

B: OK. "With All My Heart, David. Nov. 19, 1998." Oh, yes. This is it. This is your watch.

G: That's great. Could you send it to me? I'm in ^{10.}_____.

Bellboy: Yes, we can. But would you mind ⁱ¹·_____ in advance?

Guest: Sure, how much is it?

B: We'll find out, and ¹²·_____ later.

G: OK.

B: We'll send you an e-mail to tell you the amount of postage and our bank ¹³·_____. So please send the money to our bank account ¹⁴·_____. Then, we'll send you the watch. Or, ¹⁵·_____, you can send us an international postal ¹⁶·_____.

G: OK. An international postal money order is ¹⁷·_____ me. I'll send it to you.

B: Certainly, ma'am. May I have your name and your e-mail address, please?

G: Sure. My name is Mary Clark. My e-mail address is "m-a-r-y hyphen c-l-a-r-k at abcd dot com."

B: ¹⁸·_____ your e-mail address, "m-a-r-y hyphen c-l-a-r-k at abcd dot com." I'll send you an e-mail soon. If you do not receive any e-mail, please call me again. My name is Matsukawa.

G: Sure, I will. I really ¹⁹·_____ your help. I'll wait for your e-mail.

B: It's ²⁰·_____, Ms. Clark.

🧳 After Listening

Writing & Presentation

ペアを作り、部屋に忘れ物をしたゲストに、異なる状況（部屋番号、忘れ物、支払い方法など）に変更してスタッフが対応する会話を作ってみましょう。忘れ物の特徴やメールアドレスの確認をして、ゲストに確実に忘れ物を送付できるように努めましょう。そして、グループ同士で、あるいはクラス全体でプレゼンテーションしてみましょう。

Additional Listening & Comprehension Questions

2人の会話を聞き、内容に関する質問の答えとして最も適切な選択肢を選びましょう。

🎧 DL 30, 31   💿 CD 30   💿 CD 31

1. What has the guest just finished?

    a. Breakfast   b. Lunch   c. Dinner   d. Coffee

2. What did the guest enjoy at the Coffee House?

    a. Talking with her friends   b. Talking with the hotel staff
    c. Talking about her friends   d. Talking about the hotel staff

3. What's the guest's problem?

    a. She doesn't like the hotel.
    b. She has to buy souvenirs for her family and friends.
    c. She cannot communicate well with the hotel staff.
    d. She has a lot of luggage.

4. When will the bellboy come to the guest's room to collect her luggage?

    a. Before 10:30   b. At 10:30
    c. When breakfast is ready   d. When her luggage is ready

Useful Tips for Providing Hotel Services

英語で困ったら

ゲストの英語が聞き取れなかったり、英語でどのように表現して良いか分からない場合は、以下の表現を使ってコミュニケーションを継続させる努力をしてみましょう。

1. 「もう一度言ってください」と依頼する。
    I beg your pardon?   Would/Could you repeat what you said?
2. 「ゆっくり話して頂けますか」と依頼する。
    Would/Could you speak more slowly, please?
3. 相手の言ったことを正しく理解しているか確認する。
    You mean 〜, sir/ma'am?   Do you mean 〜, sir/ma'am?
    「〜ということをおっしゃっているのですね？」(You mean 以下は相手の言った内容)
4. 上記１〜３でも分からない場合は、「誰かを呼んで来ます」と言う。
    Let me call my manager.「マネジャーを呼んで参ります」
    Let me call someone who can speak better English.「英語の上手な者を呼んで参ります」
    そして、どちらかの文の後には、次の文を続けて言いましょう。
    Would/Could you wait for a moment?「少々お待ち頂けますか？」

Unit 7

Order Taking at a Restaurant: Food Description
Taking an Order for Steak

レストランでのオーダー・テイキング―料理説明／ステーキのオーダー・テイキング

🔔 Pre-Listening

Key Vocabulary

次の定義に当てはまる語句を、選択肢から選びましょう。

[   ] **1.** having a special quality, style, or attractiveness
[   ] **2.** making someone hungry
[   ] **3.** of rare excellence or beauty
[   ] **4.** fully grown or developed
[   ] **5.** soft and easy to cut or bite
[   ] **6.** to enjoy the taste of
[   ] **7.** to keep away from
[   ] **8.** to want to have something
[   ] **9.** to make a meal
[   ]**10.** to cut the amount

a. appetizing	**b.** avoid	**c.** care for	**d.** distinctive	**e.** exquisite
f. matured	**g.** prepare	**h.** reduce	**i.** savor	**j.** tender

Understanding Basic Expressions

次の基本表現の音声を聞き、どこに強勢（アクセント）を置くか確認しましょう。音声をまねて繰り返し音読し、同時に意味を考えてみましょう。

1. Would you like something to drink?
2. We have a variety of drinks, such as champagne, wine, draft beer, and non-alcoholic cocktails.
3. I'd like a glass of champagne.
4. Might I recommend the fresh Bretagne homard lobster?
5. Sounds delicious.
6. It will be boiled just until it's half done.
7. We'll serve it with bechamel sauce and vegetables in season.
8. Would you care for an appetizer?
9. We can reduce the amount of butter if you like.
10. Would you like olive oil as a substitute?

心を伝えるおもてなし表現

Might I recommend the fresh Bretagne homard lobster?
「新鮮なブルターニュ産のオマールエビはいかがでしょうか？」
ゲストが何を食べようか決めかねている時、"Might I recommend ～ ?" でお勧めのメニューを提案することができます。その際、このスキットのように十分にそのメニューが説明できるようになっておきましょう。そうすればゲストとの会話も弾み、良いサービスになります。

We can reduce the amount of butter if you like.
「（ゲストの特別な希望に応えて）もしよろしければ、バターの量を減らすこともできます」
これは、ゲストの希望に沿えるよう提案している表現です。if you like（「もしよろしければ」）は相手の希望を尊重する表現で、これがあることで全体に温かみを増しています。

Would you like olive oil as a substitute?
「代わりにオリーブ・オイルはいかがでしょうか？」
「バターを減らしたい」と希望するゲストに対し、レストラン・スタッフがオリーブ・オイルを代替品として（as a substitute）使うことを提案しています。前述のバター使用量に関する提案の表現と同様に、ゲストが言う前に希望を察知して具体的な提案をしている表現です。

While Listening

Comprehension Questions　　DL 33, 34　CD 33　CD 34

A 2人の会話を聞き、内容の順に選択肢を並べ替えましょう。

1.____ → 2.____ → 3.____ → 4.____ → 5.____ → 6.____ → 7.____ → 8.____

a. The guest asks the restaurant server about the difference between the two champagnes.
b. The guest is given the day's menu.
c. The guest chooses her champagne.
d. The guest orders the confit of the duck foie gras.
e. The guest requests that the kitchen staff use olive oil in her food.
f. The restaurant server asks the guest if she would like an appetizer.
g. The restaurant server describes the tastes of the champagnes to the guest.
h. The restaurant server recommends the Bretagne live homard lobster.

B 会話の内容に関する質問の答えとして、最も適切な選択肢を選びましょう。

1. What kind of drink does the guest order?
   a. Champagne　b. Wine　c. Non-alcoholic beer　d. Cocktails

2. What is a feature of the Louis Roederer?
   a. Rich and smooth flavors　　b. A matured taste
   c. Tender and chewy　　d. Sweet and sour flavors

3. Why does the restaurant server recommend the Bretagne homard lobster?
   a. Because it is the cheapest among homard lobsters.
   b. Because it is the best among homard lobsters.
   c. Because it is the only homard lobster available.
   d. Because it is the very homard lobster the restaurant server likes.

4. How is the homard cooked?
   a. Half-grilled　b. Well-boiled　c. Half-boiled　d. Well-grilled

5. What is served with the cooked homard?
   a. Butter sauce　b. Sour cream　c. Bechamel sauce　d. Foie gras

6. What will the guest have for an appetizer?

    a. A lobster   b. Season's vegetables   c. Champagne   d. Foie gras

7. What does the guest try to take less of these days?

    a. Butter   b. Olive oil   c. Shellfish   d. Meat

Dictation Exercise

会話をもう一度聞き、空所に語句を書き入れましょう。

🎧 DL 33   💿 CD 33

Restaurant Server: Good evening, Ms. Smith. Thank you very much for your reservation tonight. ^{1.} _____, would you like something to drink? We have a variety of drinks, such as champagne, wine, ^{2.} _____, and non-alcoholic cocktails.

Guest: I'd like ^{3.} _____ champagne. What kind of champagne do you have?

R: We have Louis Roederer Brut Premier and Piper Heidsieck Cuvee Rare.

G: How are they different?

R: Louis Roederer has an ^{4.} _____ balanced taste with ^{5.} _____ flavors, which gives a refreshing taste. And ^{6.} _____ Piper Heidsieck, you can enjoy ^{7.} _____ with rich, ^{8.} _____.

G: Then I'll have Louis Roederer.

R: Thank you very much. I will prepare your champagne. Just one moment, please.

🎧 DL 34   💿 CD 34

After the champagne is served.

Restaurant Server: Here is your champagne. This is today's menu.

Guest: Well, it's difficult to decide ^{9.} _____. Every item looks so delicious.

R: Then, might I recommend the fresh Bretagne homard lobster? Bretagne homard is the best of the homard lobsters. What makes it ^{10.} _____

is that it is tender and ⁱ¹·_____. I think you'll appreciate and ¹²·_____.

G: Sounds delicious.

R: It surely is, ma'am. We take one live homard out of the ¹³·_____ right after we get an order. Since it is a very fresh homard, it will be boiled just until it's ¹⁴·_____. We'll serve it with bechamel sauce and ¹⁵·_____.

G: Sounds good. I'll take it.

R: Thank you. And would you care for an ¹⁶·_____?

G: Let's see. I'll have the confit of the duck foie gras.

R: ¹⁷·_____, ma'am. Then, after the appetizer, we'll bring you the Bretagne homard.

G: OK. By the way, I try to ¹⁸·_____ a lot of butter these days.

R: Well, we can ¹⁹·_____ the amount of butter if you like. Or would you like olive oil ²⁰·_____?

G: Yes, please. I'd like olive oil. Thank you.

R: You're welcome.

After Listening

Writing & Presentation

ペアを作り、ゲストに「本日のお勧めドリンク、スペシャル、コース料理」などを紹介する会話を作ってみましょう。ゲストの食に関する好みやアレルギーの有無について聞き取り、それに対応する方法を自由に変更して考えてみましょう。そして、グループ同士で、あるいはクラス全体でプレゼンテーションしてみましょう。

Additional Listening & Comprehension Questions

2人の会話を聞き、内容に関する質問の答えとして最も適切な選択肢を選びましょう。

DL 35, 36　CD 35　CD 36

1. What does the guest order for dinner?
    a. Grilled chicken steak with fresh vegetables
    b. Pork fillet steak with fresh vegetables
    c. Beef rib steak with fresh vegetables
    d. Beef fillet steak with fresh vegetables

2. How does the guest like his steak cooked?
    a. Rare　b. Medium-rare　c. Medium　d. Well-done

3. What's the soup of the day?
    a. Corn soup　b. Cream soup　c. Chicken soup　d. Carrot soup

4. What drink does the guest order?
    a. Red wine　b. White wine　c. Beer　d. Whiskey

Useful Tips for Providing Hotel Services

レストランの食事は経験

ゲストがレストランで食事をするのは、宿泊と同様に一つの経験として強く印象に残ります。ゲストはレストランを選んだ時点でどのような料理やサービスがあるのか、ある程度予測しています。レストラン・スタッフはその期待に応えるだけでなく、期待以上のサービスで感動を与えなければなりません。本スキットのように、まずは、丁寧な料理の説明ができることが重要なサービスとなります。料理の材料、その産地、調理法まで詳細な知識が必要です。また、ゲストのニーズにあった食事を提供するために、時にはその日の体調や空腹具合はどれくらいか、また、前日の食事内容を聞きながら、メニューを提案する場合もあります。これらの会話によるサービスから、レストランでの食事がゲストにとって自分だけの特別な経験となるのです。

Unit 8

Order Taking at a Restaurant: Recommendations / Taking a Breakfast Order

レストランでのオーダー・テイキング—料理提案／朝食のオーダー・テイキング

Pre-Listening

Key Vocabulary

次の定義に当てはまる語句を、選択肢から選びましょう。

[　] 1. the chief cook in a restaurant or hotel
[　] 2. a kind of sea creature with a pair of flat round shells
[　] 3. having an allergy
[　] 4. the foods and spices used to make a particular dish
[　] 5. the salted eggs of a sturgeon
[　] 6. the sensations people have when they eat food or drink; preference for something
[　] 7. to be in good harmony with something
[　] 8. to cook food in an oven or over direct heat
[　] 9. to put something in a larger group
[　]10. to suggest favorably

a. allergic	**b.** caviar	**c.** chef	**d.** go well	**e.** include
f. ingredients	**g.** recommend	**h.** roast	**i.** scallop	**j.** taste

43

Understanding Basic Expressions

次の基本表現の音声を聞き、どこに強勢（アクセント）を置くか確認しましょう。音声をまねて繰り返し音読し、同時に意味を考えてみましょう。

1. May I take your order?
2. Would you like a glass of champagne or a bottle?
3. I'll be right back with your champagne.
4. How about beginning with a nice appetizer?
5. Your champagne goes well with lobster.
6. Would you like some soup while you are waiting?
7. Do you have anything you don't like to eat?
8. Are there any ingredients we should avoid?
9. I'm allergic to shellfish.
10. We'll change them to something else for you.

心を伝えるおもてなし表現

I'll be right back with your champagne.「すぐにシャンパンをお持ちします」
I'll be right back で「すぐに（間もなく）戻ってくる」という意味を示します。ゲストの気持ちを汲んで、待たせることなく早く持ってくることを効果的に伝えられる表現です。

How about beginning with a nice appetizer?
「美味しい前菜でお食事をお始めになってはいかがでしょうか？」
"How about 〜 ?" で料理を勧めています。この表現は、Unit 5 の観光地を勧める場面でも使用されています。

Would you like some soup while you are waiting?
「お待ち頂く間にスープはいかがですか？」
"Would you like 〜 ?" でスープを勧めています。Unit 7 で登場した "Would you care for 〜 ?" も同様の意味です。

Do you have anything you don't like to eat?「食べたくないもの（食材）はございますか？」
Are there any ingredients we should avoid?「私達が避けるべき材料はございますか？」
アレルギー源となる食べ物だけでなく、嫌いな食べ物、宗教上の理由により食べることが禁じられている食べ物も含めて、避けるべき食材を尋ねています。アレルギーがあるかどうか直接的に尋ねる場合の "Are you allergic to any foods?" よりも間接的な表現なので丁寧になります。

We'll change them to something else for you.
「それらをあなたのために何かほかのものに変えましょう」
このテキストで何度も出てきている for you という表現で「あなたのために」を強調しつつ、ゲストの立場になって、アレルギーがある食材を他のものに変える提案をしています。

While Listening

Comprehension Questions　　DL 38, 39 ・CD 38 ・CD 39

A 2人の会話を聞き、内容の順に選択肢を並べ替えましょう。

1.___ → 2.___ → 3.___ → 4.___ → 5.___ → 6.___ → 7.___ → 8.___

a. The guest gets the menu for the day.
b. The guest orders a glass of champagne.
c. The guest orders potage soup.
d. The guest orders roasted duck.
e. The guest says that he is allergic to shellfish.
f. The restaurant server recommends "Lobster Salad with Caviar" for an appetizer.
g. The restaurant server says that she will ask the kitchen not to use garlic in the guest's dish.
h. The restaurant server suggests changing scallops to some other ingredients.

B 会話の内容に関する質問の答えとして、最も適切な選択肢を選びましょう。

1. What is the guest's name?
   a. Smith　b. Brown　c. Kim　d. Taylor

2. What kind of drink does the guest have?
   a. A bottle of wine
   b. A glass of wine
   c. A bottle of champagne
   d. A glass of champagne

3. What does the guest order for his main dish?
   a. Roasted duck
   b. Baked salmon
   c. Roasted pork
   d. Grilled chicken

4. What is the guest allergic to?
   a. Eggs　b. Peanuts　c. Shellfish　d. Garlic

5. What is another request of the guest?
   a. He wants to have dinner right away.
   b. He wants to avoid salt.
   c. He doesn't want garlic in his food.
   d. He wants to have more garlic.

6. What is the restaurant's policy?
   a. To make the guests happy
   b. To make a lot of profits
   c. To make the restaurant popular
   d. To suit the guests' needs and tastes

Dictation Exercise

会話をもう一度聞き、空所に語句を書き入れましょう。

🎧 DL 38   💿 CD 38

Restaurant Server: Good evening, Mr. Brown. May I ¹·_____ _____ ?

Guest: Sure. Do you have champagne?

R: ²·_____, Mr. Brown. Would you like a glass of champagne or ³·_____?

G: A glass, please.

R: Thank you very much. I'll be ⁴·_____ your champagne. ⁵·_____, please.

A few minutes later.

R: Here is your champagne. And this is ⁶·_____ tonight.

G: Thank you. And, this champagne is delicious ⁷·_____!

R: Thank you very much. This champagne is rich and has a well-balanced and exquisite taste. ⁸·_____ you like it. Now, ⁹·_____ _____ with a nice appetizer to go with your champagne?

🎧 DL 39   💿 CD 39

Guest: OK, what ¹⁰·_____?

Restaurant Server: We have "Lobster Salad with Caviar." Your champagne ¹¹·_____ with lobster.

G: ¹²·_____. I'll have that.

R: Certainly, thank you very much.

G: And I'll take the ¹³·_____ for my main dish.

R: Well, it will ¹⁴·_____ to prepare the roasted duck. Would you like some soup while you are waiting?

G: That's ¹⁵._____. Then, potage soup, please.

R: Certainly, sir. Do you have anything you don't like to eat, or are there any ¹⁶._____ we should avoid?

G: Well, I'm ¹⁷._____ shellfish.

R: Certainly, sir. Since the appetizer includes scallops, we'll change them to something else ¹⁸._____.

G: Oh, thank you.

R: You're very welcome, sir.

G: And, I don't like garlic very much.

R: Certainly, sir. I'll ¹⁹._____ to use garlic in your dish.

G: That's wonderful. Thank you very much.

R: You're quite welcome. It is our restaurant's policy to suit our guests' ²⁰._____.

After Listening

Writing & Presentation

ペアを作り、卵アレルギーがあるゲストがレストランで注文するという設定で会話を作ってみましょう。卵が含まれていない料理の中でゲストの好みに合うものを適切に勧めてみましょう。そして、グループ同士で、あるいはクラス全体でプレゼンテーションしてみましょう。

Additional Listening & Comprehension Questions

2人の会話を聞き、内容に関する質問の答えとして最も適切な選択肢を選びましょう。

1. What kind of breakfast does the guest have?
   a. Japanese   b. Chinese   c. American   d. Continental

2. What kind of juice does the guest have?
   a. Orange   b. Tomato   c. Apple   d. Grapefruit

3. How does the guest want her egg cooked?
   a. Poached   b. Over hard   c. Fried   d. Scrambled

4. What does the guest want with the egg?
   a. Ham   b. Bacon   c. Sausage   d. Salad

Useful Tips for Providing Hotel Services

オーダーの取り方で売り上げアップ

Unit 8 では、料理のオーダーを取る担当者は、お勧めの料理を提案したり、追加のオーダーになり得るメニュー（飲み物、前菜、スープ、サラダ、デザートなど）の中から前菜やスープを勧めています。本スキットでは、「時間のかかる料理を待つ間にスープはいかがですか？」と実にタイミング良く提案しています。また、レストランでは通常、メイン・ディッシュを出した後、しばらくたってから、"How is everything?"「（全てを含んで）いかがでしょうか？」と聞きます。これは、料理が希望通り調理されているか（ステーキの焼き方やアレルギー対応など）、味はどうか、さらにレストランの環境（空調、テーブル周り）などの感想や意見を聞くもので、何か問題があればすぐに対応するというサービスの姿勢を示すものでもあります。また、飲み物の追加など、さらなるオーダーを生むきっかけにもなり、セールス的な機能を果たす表現にもなります（この "How is[was] everything?" は全ての部署の様々な状況で使用できる表現です）。このように、レストラン・サービスの担当者は、売り上げをアップさせる意識とテクニックも求められているのです。

Restaurant Reservations
Handling a Complaint: Misunderstanding Words

レストラン予約／苦情対応―言葉の聞き間違い

 Pre-Listening

Key Vocabulary

次の定義に当てはまる語句を、選択肢から選びましょう。

[ ] 1. a group of people
[ ] 2. extremely good
[ ] 3. someone who is staying in a hotel
[ ] 4. to become a member of a group
[ ] 5. to expect that something good will happen
[ ] 6. to give something to someone
[ ] 7. to like something better than something else
[ ] 8. to make certain of something
[ ] 9. to make plans and reservations
[ ]10. to be obtained at a particular price

a. arrange	**b.** cost	**c.** guest	**d.** great	**e.** join
f. look forward to	**g.** make sure	**h.** party	**i.** prefer	**j.** provide

49

Understanding Basic Expressions

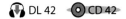

次の基本表現の音声を聞き、どこに強勢（アクセント）を置くか確認しましょう。音声をまねて繰り返し音読し、同時に意味を考えてみましょう。

1. How many people are in your party?
2. What time will you be joining us?
3. Would you prefer smoking or non-smoking?
4. We are celebrating my daughter's birthday.
5. We're glad to serve you on her special day.
6. It's exactly the right size for four people.
7. It costs only 3,000 yen.
8. Is anybody allergic to any foods?
9. My son has an allergy to peanuts.
10. I'll ask our chef not to use peanuts in your dinner.

心を伝えるおもてなし表現

What time will you be joining us?「何時にお越しになりますか？」
レストランへのゲストの到着時間を尋ねています。us はレストランのスタッフ全体のことで、これから楽しい時間を共有する近しい人々を意味し、join（「加わる」）という単語とともに、この表現全体にフレンドリーなサービスや丁寧さを生み出しています。同様の表現で、"What time can we expect you?" も使いますが、おもてなしの観点では、この "What time will you be joining us?" の方がより温かみがある表現です。

We're glad to serve you on her special day.
「彼女の特別な日にあなた方にサービスすることができ、私達は嬉しいです」
この表現は、子供の誕生日を祝うゲストの嬉しい気持ちをスタッフも共有していることを伝えています。

It costs only 3,000 yen.「わずか3,000円でございます」
商品の値段を言う表現は、"It costs 〜." あるいは "It is 〜." ですが、値段の数字の前に only を入れることで、値ごろ感や手ごろ感を表現しています。日本語のセールス・トークでも「わずか（たったの）〜円です」がよく使われるのと同様です。

Do you have any other requests?「他にご要望はございますか？」
この表現でゲストの要望に積極的に答えようとする姿勢を表現することができます。これと同様の表現は、Unit 1 の客室に対する要望を聞く場面で登場しています。

While Listening

Comprehension Questions 　DL 43, 44　　CD 43　　CD 44

A 2人の会話を聞き、内容の順に選択肢を並べ替えましょう。

1.___ → 2.___ → 3.___ → 4.___ → 5.___ → 6.___ → 7.___ → 8.___

a. The guest orders a special birthday cake.
b. The guest reserves a window-side table.
c. The guest tells the restaurant server that she will come to the restaurant at 7:30 the next day.
d. The restaurant server asks about any food allergies in the guest's party.
e. The restaurant server asks the guest her daughter's name and age.
f. The restaurant server asks the guest the number of persons in her party.
g. The restaurant server asks the guest's name.
h. The restaurant server confirms the reservation.

B 会話の内容に関する質問の答えとして、最も適切な選択肢を選びましょう。

1. Who is Brenda Wilson?
   a. A hotel concierge　b. A guest　c. A chef　d. A restaurant employee

2. How many people will come to the dinner?
   a. Three　b. Four　c. Five　d. Unknown

3. What is the dinner for?
   a. Brenda's birthday　　　　b. Brenda's wedding anniversary
   c. Brenda's daughter's birthday　d. Brenda's son's birthday

4. When is the cake expected to be served?
   a. Before dinner　　　　b. After dinner
   c. After they leave　　　d. Right now

5. What kind of request does the guest make?
   a. A table by the window　　　b. A table near the entrance
   c. A special room for the party　d. A special dinner course for the party

6. Who has an allergy to peanuts?
   a. Brenda　b. Brenda's son　c. Brenda's daughter　d. Nobody

Dictation Exercise

会話をもう一度聞き、空所に語句を書き入れましょう。

🎧 DL 43 💿 CD 43

Restaurant Server: Good afternoon. This is Happy Bistro, Yamada speaking. How may I help you?

Guest: Hello, Mr. Yamada. Could I ¹._____ for tomorrow evening?

R: Yes, ma'am. May I ²._____, please?

G: Brenda Wilson.

R: Ms. Wilson, are you a ³._____ of this hotel?

G: Yes, my room number is 2302.

R: Thank you very much, Ms. Wilson. How many people are ⁴._____ _____?

G: There will be four tomorrow evening.

R: And what time will you ⁵._____, ma'am?

G: At 7:30.

R: Would you ⁶._____ smoking or non-smoking?

G: Non-smoking, please. And we are ⁷._____ my daughter's birthday.

R: Oh, great! Ms. Wilson. We're ⁸._____ serve you on her special day.

🎧 DL 44 💿 CD 44

Guest: Thank you. I heard this restaurant provides excellent food and service, so we decided to come here for her birthday dinner.

Restaurant Server: Thank you very much, Ms. Wilson. ⁹._____, we can arrange the chef's special birthday cake for dessert. It's exactly the ¹⁰._____ size for four people and it ¹¹._____ only 3,000 yen.

G: That ¹²._____ nice. I'll order it now.

R: Thank you very much, Ms. Wilson. Our chef will write a message for your daughter on the birthday cake. May I ask your daughter's name and her age?

G: Sure. Her name is Audrey, and she will be 16 tomorrow.

R: Could you spell out your daughter's name?

G: Of course. It's A-U-D-R-E-Y, Audrey.

R: ¹³._____. The message will be "Happy Birthday, Audrey. Sweet 16!" How is that?

G: Yes, sounds wonderful.

R: Thank you, ma'am. Do you have any other ¹⁴._____?

G: Can I ¹⁵._____ a window-side table?

R: Certainly, ma'am. I'll reserve a table ¹⁶._____ for your party.

G: Thank you.

R: You're very welcome. Is anybody allergic to any foods? Are there any ingredients we should avoid?

G: Oh, my son ¹⁷._____ to peanuts.

R: Certainly, ma'am. I'll ask our chef not to use peanuts ¹⁸._____ _____.

G: Thank you very much.

R: Now, ¹⁹._____ your reservation. That's a reservation for Ms. Wilson for four people, non-smoking at 7:30 tomorrow evening. We'll make sure there are no peanuts.

G: That's correct.

R: Thank you. We are ²⁰._____ seeing you then, Ms. Wilson.

G: Thank you, Mr. Yamada. Good-by.

📋 After Listening

Writing & Presentation

ペアを作り、ゲストがレストラン・スタッフを相手にレストランを予約する会話を作ってみましょう。ゲストの名前、部屋番号、予約を希望する日時、予約人数、食物アレルギーの有無、特別な要望などを自由に変更して考えてみましょう。レストラン・スタッフはゲストからの要望に対して、ゲストをより満足させる提案をするよう心がけましょう。そして、グループ同士で、あるいはクラス全体でプレゼンテーションしてみましょう。

Additional Listening & Comprehension Questions

2人の会話を聞き、内容に関する質問の答えとして最も適切な選択肢を選びましょう。

DL 45, 46 ・CD 45 ・CD 46

1. What did the guest order from Room Service?

    a. Fruit   b. Cakes   c. Drinks   d. Salads

2. What does the guest's daughter have an allergy to?

    a. Melon   b. Watermelon   c. Fruit   d. Eggs

3. What seems to have caused the guest's problem?

    a. The guest's misunderstanding
    b. The guest's daughter's carelessness
    c. The order taker's misunderstanding
    d. The order taker's forgetfulness

4. Who will the guest talk to on the phone?

    a. The front desk manager   b. The restaurant manager
    c. The room service manager   d. The general manager

Useful Tips for Providing Hotel Services

パーソナル・サービス―アレルギー等への対応―

ゲストの好みや希望に合わせるサービスは、パーソナル・サービスと呼ばれ、顧客満足度を高くすると言われています。パーソナル・サービスにより、大勢のゲストのうちの1人としてではなく、特別なゲストとして大切に応対されたという気持ちにさせるからです。食物アレルギーが珍しいことではなくなった現代では、レストランにおけるアレルギーへの対応は重要なパーソナル・サービスの一つです。そのためには、レストランとしてどこまでゲストのニーズに応える用意があるのかをスタッフ全てが認識していることが重要です。Unit 8 と Unit 9 のスキットでは、レストラン・スタッフはゲストのアレルギー源となる食材や嫌いな食材を使わないと言っていますが、シェフをはじめとする調理場スタッフがそういった対応をすることを予め承知しているから迅速に対応できたことです。また、卵など、主なアレルギー源となりうる食材が含まれる料理については、調理場のスタッフから情報を聞いて知識を蓄え、代替のメニューをはじめ、いつでも適切な料理の提案ができるようになっていることが大切です。

Unit 10

At the Gift Shop
Handling a Complaint: "No Rolls!"

ギフト・ショップにて／苦情対応—ロールパンがない！

Pre-Listening

Key Vocabulary

次の定義に当てはまる語句を、選択肢から選びましょう。

[   ] 1. a member of the hotel staff in charge of special services for guests
[   ] 2. having no faults or damage
[   ] 3. one of a pair of thin sticks used for picking up food
[   ] 4. products that someone makes in a skillful way
[   ] 5. something kept as a reminder of a place, person, or occasion
[   ] 6. to coat something using a traditional Japanese technique
[   ] 7. to cover something completely with paper or cloth
[   ] 8. to record the cost of something in an account
[   ] 9. to write one's name
[   ]10. writing materials such as paper and envelopes

a. charge	**b.** chopstick	**c.** concierge	**d.** craft	**e.** lacquer
f. perfect	**g.** sign	**h.** souvenir	**i.** stationery	**j.** wrap

55

Understanding Basic Expressions

次の基本表現の音声を聞き、どこに強勢（アクセント）を置くか確認しましょう。音声をまねて繰り返し音読し、同時に意味を考えてみましょう。

1. We have a variety of foods perfect for gifts.
2. What about our cookies and fruit cakes?
3. Many international guests buy them for themselves as well as their family and friends.
4. Your bill comes to 5,940 yen.
5. Can I charge this to my room?
6. Could you write down your room number and your name, and sign here, please?
7. Could you tell me where I can buy Japanese crafts for souvenirs?
8. You can buy many kinds of beautiful crafts such as chopsticks, traditional wrapping cloths called *furoshiki*, or black-lacquered boxes.
9. If you'd like a map to the department stores, you can get one at the concierge desk.
10. I hope you will enjoy shopping and have a nice day!

 心を伝えるおもてなし表現

How are you?「ご機嫌いかがでしょうか？」
この表現は英語学習の初期に誰もが習うものですが、英語でのコミュニケーションや人間関係構築にとってとても重要な表現です。本来は相手の体調を気遣う表現ですが、あまりにも慣用的に使われているので、その詳しい返事をあまり期待せず、挨拶の決まり文句のように使われる場合もよくあります。いつでも、誰にでも使えますので、"Good morning!" などの挨拶の後、すぐに続けてこの表現を使ってみましょう。また、特に相手の体調が優れないことを知っている場合は、"How are you feeling?"（「ご気分はいかがですか？」）という表現で尋ねます。状況に合わせて、正しく使い分けましょう。

If you'd like a map to the department stores, you can get one at the concierge desk.
「デパートへの地図でしたら、コンシェルジュにあります」
デパートに行くというゲストに対して、ゲストのニーズを先に察知して提案しています。

I hope you will enjoy shopping and have a nice day!
「お買い物を楽しんで、良い一日をお過ごしください」
同様の表現は Unit 2 でも解説しましたが、本 Unit のスキットのように enjoy の後に動詞の ing 形を続ければ、「〜することを楽しんでください」ということを表現できます。

While Listening

Comprehension Questions DL 48, 49   CD 48   CD 49

A 2人の会話を聞き、内容の順に選択肢を並べ替えましょう。

1.____ → 2.____ → 3.____ → 4.____ → 5.____ → 6.____ → 7.____ → 8.____

a. The guest asks the shop clerk if he can charge the bill to his room.
b. The guest decides to buy the cookies and fruit cakes.
c. The guest is looking for good foods for his family and friends.
d. The guest signs the bill.
e. The guest wants to know a good store that sells Japanese crafts.
f. The shop clerk tells the guest he can get a map at the concierge desk.
g. The shop clerk recommends cookies and fruit cakes to the guest.
h. The shop clerk recommends department stores for crafts.

B 会話の内容に関する質問の答えとして、最も適切な選択肢を選びましょう。

1. What is the guest looking for at the gift shop?
   a. Maps   b. Souvenirs   c. Crafts   d. Stationery

2. What is not recommended by the shop clerk as a souvenir?
   a. Cookies   b. Cakes   c. Foods   d. Maps

3. How much is the total amount of the bill?
   a. 5,914 yen   b. 5,940 yen   c. 9,514 yen   d. 9,540 yen

4. How does the guest pay for the food at the gift shop?
   a. Charging it to his room   b. Cash   c. Credit card   d. Traveler's checks

5. Where are Japanese crafts sold?
   a. At the gift shop   b. At the hotel
   c. In a department store   d. At a station

6. Which is not mentioned as a Japanese craft by the shop clerk?
   a. Chopsticks   b. Wrapping cloths
   c. Black-lacquered boxes   d. Stationery goods

7. Who loves Japanese stationery goods?
   a. Tourists from foreign countries
   b. The shop clerk
   c. Japanese craftsmen
   d. The concierge

8. How will the guest spend the afternoon?
   a. He will buy a map.
   b. He will go to a gift shop.
   c. He will go to department stores.
   d. He will go sightseeing.

Dictation Exercise

会話をもう一度聞き、空所に語句を書き入れましょう。

DL 48　CD 48

Shop Clerk: Good afternoon, sir. 1._____ today?

Guest: Good afternoon. I'm looking for some good 2._____ for my family and friends.

S: Are you looking for any foods? We have 3._____ foods perfect for gifts.

G: Actually, I'm 4._____ good foods. My family and friends like to enjoy good foods from Japan.

S: Oh, I see! Then, 5._____ our cookies and fruit cakes? They are really delicious and many international guests buy them 6._____ as well as their family and friends.

G: Really? Oh, they 7._____ so good. Then, I'll buy three 8._____ _____ cookies and two small boxes of fruit cakes.

S: Thank you very much. Your bill comes to 5,940 yen.

G: Can I 9._____ this to my room?

S: Certainly, sir. Could you 10._____ your room number and your name, and sign here, please?

G: Sure.

S: Thank you very much, sir.

Guest: By the way, [11]_____ tell me where I can buy Japanese crafts for souvenirs?

Shop Clerk: If you go to a department store, you can buy many [12]_____ of beautiful crafts [13]_____ chopsticks, traditional wrapping cloths called *furoshiki*, or black-lacquered boxes. You can also buy Japanese stationery goods, which are very popular [14]_____ international tourists.

G: Oh, that's a good idea. Thanks. I'll [15]_____ some department stores this afternoon.

S: If [16]_____ a map to the department stores, you can [17]_____ the concierge desk.

G: Thank you for [18]_____.

S: You're welcome. I hope you will enjoy shopping and [19]_____ a nice day!

G: Thank you. [20]_____.

After Listening

Writing & Presentation

ペアを作り、土産品をゲストに提案する会話を作ってみましょう。土産品の種類、内容、値段、支払方法などを自由に変更して考えてみましょう。ショップで取り扱っていない土産品についてゲストから聞かれたら、どこでそれを購入できるか親切に教えてあげましょう。そして、グループ同士で、あるいはクラス全体でプレゼンテーションしてみましょう。

Additional Listening & Comprehension Questions

2人の会話を聞き、内容に関する質問の答えとして最も適切な選択肢を選びましょう。

 DL 50, 51　　CD 50　　CD 51

1. What did the guest buy at the shop in the morning?

    a. Bread　b. Milk　c. Fruits　d. Gifts

2. What does the guest's son like the best?

    a. Cheese rolls　b. Fruit rolls　c. Butter rolls　d. Raisin rolls

3. What was the problem with the guest's raisin rolls?

    a. They were rotten.　　　　b. They were sold out.
    c. They were missing.　　　 d. They were expensive.

4. How many rolls does the guest get for free?

    a. One　b. Two　c. Three　d. Four

Useful Tips for Providing Hotel Services

サービスのプロは「幸せな人」

「幸せな人」(Happy Person) は、機嫌が良く、明るくにこやかで、元気で機敏に動きます。サービスのプロはこのような「幸せな人」ばかりです。ゲストは誰も、不機嫌な人に応対してもらいたいと思うはずはなく、快く依頼に応じてくれそうな人の方が好ましいからです。言い換えれば、「幸せな人」であるということは、サービスをする際の大前提であり、Friendly Service にとっても非常に重要なのです。しかしながら、接客現場で常に「幸せな人」でいることは困難なこともあるでしょう。日々の生活の中で辛いことや悲しいことがあったり、病気ではなくとも寝不足だったり体調が悪いこともあります。そんな時でも、現場に出れば、にこやかな笑顔をふりまける強い体力と精神力を備えた人がプロのサービス担当者です。一方で、心の中がどしゃぶりでも笑顔でサービスしていると、あら不思議、心の中が本当に晴れて軽やかになることも多いのです。「幸せな人」の素敵なサービスは、ゲストを幸せにし、そして、それがまた大きな喜びとなってスタッフ自身に戻ってくるのです。

Unit 11

Handling a Complaint at the Front Desk: Changing the Room / Bathroom Trouble

フロントでの苦情対応—ルーム・チェンジ／トイレ故障

Pre-Listening

Key Vocabulary

次の定義に当てはまる語句を、選択肢から選びましょう。

[　] 1. a disease that causes difficulties in breathing
[　] 2. a ticket or coupon
[　] 3. good enough to be considered satisfactory
[　] 4. of the present time
[　] 5. reduction in the price of something
[　] 6. to present something to someone who will decide
[　] 7. unable to be relaxed for some reason
[　] 8. a feeling of warm hospitality, e. g., providing a free gift
[　] 9. without any delay
[　]10. worried about something

a. acceptable	**b.** asthma	**c.** compliments	**d.** concerned	**e.** current
f. discount	**g.** immediately	**h.** offer	**i.** uncomfortable	**j.** voucher

Understanding Basic Expressions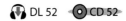

次の基本表現の音声を聞き、どこに強勢（アクセント）を置くか確認しましょう。音声をまねて繰り返し音読し、同時に意味を考えてみましょう。

1. I booked a non-smoking room.
2. We are very sorry to have made this mistake.
3. It's the same room type at the same rate.
4. Is that acceptable?
5. I'm more concerned about my health.
6. Unfortunately we have a policy to give no discounts for any rooms of the same rate.
7. We'd like to offer you a free drink voucher for our Happy Bar.
8. Please enjoy it with our compliments.
9. I'll send a bellboy immediately for your luggage.
10. I will check exactly where the noisy room is and ask them to turn it down immediately.

 心を伝えるおもてなし表現

We are very sorry to have made this mistake.「手違いがあり、誠に申し訳ございません」
間違いを詫びる表現です。手違いがあった時に広く使える表現です。

Is that acceptable?「ご了承頂けますか？」
こちら側の提案・方針・規則などをゲストに受け入れて頂かなくてはならない時に使います。

Unfortunately we have a policy to give no discounts for any rooms of the same rate.
「残念ながら、私達のホテルでは同じ料金のお部屋には割引をしないという方針です」
unfortunately（「残念ながら」）を文頭で言うと、I'm afraid（Unit 1、Unit 3、Unit 13 参照）と同様に、相手にとって都合の悪いこと、相手の要望に沿えないことを示唆し、その残念な気持ちに寄り添っていることを表現できます。また、we have a policy または it's our policy はこちら側の方針や規則を表現する時に使います。

Please enjoy it with our compliments.
「私達の贈り物（本スキットの場合は無料ドリンク券）でゆっくりおくつろぎください」
compliments は温かいおもてなしの心で特別なサービスを提供する際に使います。

Have a good evening.「良い夕べをお過ごしください」
Unit 3 と Unit 10 に出てきた "Have a nice day." は日中で、この表現は夕方以降に相手の幸せや楽しい時間を願う表現です。

While Listening

Comprehension Questions 🎧 DL 53, 54　💿 CD 53　💿 CD 54

A 2人の会話を聞き、内容の順に選択肢を並べ替えましょう。

1.___ → 2.___ → 3.___ → 4.___ → 5.___ → 6.___ → 7.___ → 8.___

a. The front desk clerk looks for another room available for the guest.
b. The front desk clerk offers the guest a ticket for a free drink.
c. The front desk clerk promises that she will solve the noise problem.
d. The front desk clerk says that she will send a bellboy immediately.
e. The front desk clerk tells the guest that he will not enjoy a nice view from the new room.
f. The guest asks the front desk clerk to give him a discount.
g. The guest complains of noise coming from a room close to his.
h. The guest complains that his room is not non-smoking.

B 会話の内容に関する質問の答えとして、最も適切な選択肢を選びましょう。

1. How did the guest make the hotel reservation?
   a. Via the Internet　　　b. By phone
   c. Through a travel agency　　　d. By fax

2. Where is the guest staying when he makes the first call to the Front Desk?
   a. In a room without a nice view　　　b. In a noisy room
   c. In a smoking room　　　d. In a non-smoking room

3. What will happen when the guest moves to his new room?
   a. He will not enjoy a nice view.　　　b. He will have to pay an extra charge.
   c. His health will be damaged.　　　d. He will enjoy smoking.

4. What is the guest's new room number?
   a. 1519　b. 1530　c. 1531　d. 1513

5. What complimentary gift does the guest get?
   a. A nice view from his room　　　b. A discount on his room
   c. A ticket for a free drink　　　d. An upgrade of his room

6. How will the noise problem be solved?
   a. The front desk clerk will ask the guests to turn it down.
   b. The guest will go to the room and make a complaint.
   c. The problem will be solved naturally.
   d. The problem will not be solved.

Dictation Exercise

会話をもう一度聞き、空所に語句を書き入れましょう。

DL 53　CD 53

Front Desk Clerk: Good afternoon, this is the Front Desk, Harada speaking. How may I help you?

Guest: Good afternoon, Ms. Harada. I ¹._____ a non-smoking room, but my room is a smoking room. I made a reservation through the online reservation system.

F: We are ²._____ have made this mistake. Can I have your room number?

G: Room 1519. I hate to stay in smoking rooms ³._____ my asthma. Can I move to a non-smoking room immediately?

F: ⁴._____, please. Yes, Mr. Cooper, I can make a room change to room 1530 on the same floor. It's the same room type at the same rate, but you ⁵._____ as nice a view as in your current room. Is that ⁶._____, Mr. Cooper?

G: Well, I ⁷._____ if I can't have a nice view or not, as I'm ⁸._____ my health. So, it's acceptable. But since I'm not getting a similar view, can I ⁹._____?

F: Unfortunately we have a ¹⁰._____ to give no discounts for any rooms of the same rate. We're so sorry this happened. We'd ¹¹._____ offer you a free drink voucher for our Happy Bar. Please enjoy it with our compliments.

G: Oh, that's very ¹²._____ you. All right. I understand. Then, can I move to the room ¹³._____?

F: Certainly, Mr. Cooper. I'll send a bellboy immediately ¹⁴._____

_____. Your new room will be 1530.

G: Thank you very much for your understanding and quick action.

F: It's my pleasure, Mr. Cooper. I hope you will ^{15.} _____ in your new room.

G: Of course, I will. Thank you.

F: Have a good day, Mr. Cooper.

G: The same to you!

🎧 DL 54 💿 CD 54

Later in the evening.

Guest: Good evening.

Front Desk Clerk: Good evening, sir. ^{16.} _____ help you?

G: Yes. I like my new room. But, the room ^{17.} _____ next door is making a lot of noise with TV and music. I feel very uncomfortable about it.

F: I'm sorry about this. Which room is it, sir?

G: Since my room is 1530, it must be room 1531. Could you call them about the noise?

F: Yes, Mr. Cooper, ^{18.} _____ exactly where the noisy room is and ask them to turn it down immediately.

G: Thank you for your help.

F: You're welcome, Mr. Cooper. ^{19.} _____ you will enjoy your stay.

G: I'm sure I will. Thank you.

F: Have ^{20.} _____, Mr. Cooper.

G: You, too!

📋 After Listening

Writing & Presentation

ペアを作り、ゲストがフロント・スタッフに対して客室に関する苦情を訴える会話を作ってみましょう。苦情の内容について自由に考えてみましょう。ゲストから出た苦情についてその原因を説明し、ゲストの要望を聞いて適切に応対しましょう。そして、グループ同士で、あるいはクラス全体でプレゼンテーションしてみましょう。

Additional Listening & Comprehension Questions

2人の会話を聞き、内容に関する質問の答えとして最も適切な選択肢を選びましょう。

🎧 DL 55, 56   💿 CD 55   💿 CD 56

1. What's the guest's room number?
   a. 2011   b. 1112   c. 1211   d. 2012

2. What happens to the toilet in the guest's room?
   a. The water doesn't run.   b. The door doesn't close.
   c. The water doesn't stop.   d. The fan doesn't work.

3. What's the problem with the TV set?
   a. The guest can't find it.   b. The guest can't turn it on.
   c. The guest can't turn it around.   d. The guest can't move it.

4. When will the technician come to the guest's room?
   a. Later   b. In the afternoon   c. Soon   d. Never

Useful Tips for Providing Hotel Services

苦情の対応について

苦情が発生した時、どのように対処すれば良いでしょうか？お詫びをしなければいけないことは分かるけれど、どのようにそれを伝えれば良いのか、最初は誰でも悩むものです。ゲストが苦情を訴えたら、まずは、相手の主張をしっかり聞くことです。これはどんな新人でもできることです。それから、相手の目を見て、心からお詫びをします。そして、原因や事情を調査して説明し、できるだけ相手の希望を聞き入れて対処を行います。一般的な苦情を収める方法としては、「人」、「時間」、「場所」の3つを変えることが重要と言われています。例えば、人を変える場合はより熟練した人、上司、支配人などが代わって応対する、時間を変える場合は翌日にまた話をする、場所を変える場合は静かに話せる別室に通す、謝罪に自宅を訪問するなどです。このような方法で苦情に真摯に対応していくことで、ゲストの怒りが収まるきっかけも次第に生まれてきます。さらに、もし適切に対処できれば、苦情を訴えたゲストは後にそのホテルに愛着を感じ、常連客になる場合も多いものです。適切で迅速な苦情対応は様々な意味で大きなチャンスとも言われる所以です。

Unit 12

Handling a Complaint at a Restaurant: Order Problems
"Where Is My Lunch?"

レストランでの苦情対応―特別料理注文／私のランチはどこ？

🔔 Pre-Listening

Key Vocabulary

次の定義に当てはまる語句を、選択肢から選びましょう。

[   ] 1. a group of things from which a choice may be made
[   ] 2. absence of something
[   ] 3. achievable, feasible
[   ] 4. an arrangement to do something in the future
[   ] 5. not as good as expected
[   ] 6. prepared and set for action
[   ] 7. something that does not follow a rule
[   ] 8. to provide food or drink at a restaurant or bar
[   ] 9. to tell someone officially about something
[   ]10. to tolerate

| a. booking | b. disappointing | c. exception | d. inform | e. lack |
| f. possible | g. ready | h. selection | i. serve | j. stand |

Understanding Basic Expressions

次の基本表現の音声を聞き、どこに強勢（アクセント）を置くか確認しましょう。音声をまねて繰り返し音読し、同時に意味を考えてみましょう。

1. Table for one?
2. Unfortunately all the window seats are occupied at the moment.
3. I don't mind having a table away from the window.
4. It's only available if you order at least two days in advance.
5. Let me ask the manager about it.
6. The "Fuji Course" can't be prepared because of a lack of ingredients.
7. That's why we need two days' advance booking.
8. Which dinner course would you like to order, "Sakura" or "Toki"?
9. A selection of desserts will be brought for you to choose from.
10. Would you like to have a cup of coffee, tea, or something else with dessert?

心を伝えるおもてなし表現

Let me see.「そうですね」
返事を考えている時や、自分の考えをまとめている間に言う表現です。"Well." も同様の意味で、両者ともに考える時間が欲しい時に必ず言うようにしましょう。黙って考えていると、ゲストに自分が言ったことが分からなかったのかと勘違いされ、ゲストが困惑しますので注意しましょう。

Unfortunately all the window seats are occupied at the moment.
「あいにく、現在、窓側の席は全て満席です」
Unit 11 でも unfortunately について解説しましたが、文頭につけて言うことで、ゲストの残念に思う気持ちに寄り添っています。

Not at all, sir.「どういたしまして」
男性ゲストからの "Thank you." に対する返事のバリエーションの一つです。女性ゲストの場合は、"Not at all, ma'am." になります。

Would you like to have a cup of coffee, tea, or something else with dessert?
「デザートとご一緒にコーヒー、紅茶、または、何か他のお飲み物はいかがですか？」
デザートを注文したゲストに飲み物を勧める表現です。something else は「何か他のもの」という意味で、この文では他の飲み物を総称して示しています。

While Listening

Comprehension Questions　🎧 DL 58, 59　💿 CD 58　💿 CD 59

A 2人の会話を聞き、内容の順に選択肢を並べ替えましょう。

1.____ → 2.____ → 3.____ → 4.____ → 5.____ → 6.____ → 7.____ → 8.____

- a. The guest asks for a non-smoking table.
- b. The guest chooses a fillet steak for the main dish.
- c. The guest orders a cup of cappuccino.
- d. The guest orders the "Sakura Course."
- e. The guest tries to order the "Fuji Course."
- f. The restaurant server says that a table is available for the guest.
- g. The restaurant server tells the guest that no window tables are available.
- h. The restaurant server tells the guest that the "Fuji Course" is not available without an advance booking.

B 会話の内容に関する質問の答えとして、最も適切な選択肢を選びましょう。

1. What kind of table does the guest want?
   - a. A table in the smoking area
   - b. A table in the non-smoking area
   - c. A table by the window in the smoking area
   - d. No preference

2. What should guests do to have the "Fuji Course"?
   - a. They should order it a couple of days in advance.
   - b. They should order it a couple of hours in advance.
   - c. They should order it at the Front Desk just before they come to the restaurant.
   - d. They need not do anything.

3. Which course does the guest ask for and want an exception for?
   - a. The "Fuji Course"
   - b. The "Sakura Course"
   - c. The "Toki Course"
   - d. The "Fujiyama Course"

Unit 12 | 69

4. What comes after the main dish is served?

    a. Abalone   b. Fillet steak   c. Dessert   d. Soup

5. What kind of drink would the guest like with dessert?

    a. Water   b. Tea   c. Alcohol   d. Cappuccino

Dictation Exercise

会話をもう一度聞き、空所に語句を書き入れましょう。

🎧 DL 58 💿 CD 58

Restaurant Server: Good evening, sir.

Guest: Good evening.

R: 1. _____?

G: Yes. But I 2. _____ the smoking area. Can I have a table in the non-smoking area?

R: Yes, sir.

G: And I'd prefer a table by the window if possible.

R: 3. _____. Unfortunately all the window seats are 4. _____ at the moment. It may take 20 to 30 minutes to get one for you. Can you 5. _____ wait?

G: Well, I don't like to wait, so I 6. _____ a table away from the window.

R: Certainly, sir. I'll check and 7. _____ you immediately when one is available. Please wait for a few minutes, sir.

G: Thank you.

R: 8. _____, sir.

A few minutes later.

R: 9. _____ waiting. Your table is ready. 10. _____ _____ to it now.

G: Thank you.

A few minutes later.

Restaurant Server: Are you ⁱ¹· _____ order?

Guest: Yes. I would like to have a special dinner course. Can I have the "Fuji Course"?

R: I'm ¹²· _____ this, but it's only available if you order ¹³· _____ two days in advance.

G: Really? Can't you ¹⁴· _____ for me?

R: Well, let me ask the manager about it.

A few minutes later.

R: Thank you for waiting, sir. ¹⁵· _____ the manager, the "Fuji Course" can't be prepared because of a lack of ingredients. That's why we need two days' advance ¹⁶· _____. So unfortunately we can't serve it to you this evening.

G: Well, that's ¹⁷· _____. Are there any other special dinner courses available? How about "Sakura" or "Toki"?

R: Yes, either one of them is available. Which dinner course would you like to order, "Sakura" or "Toki"?

G: All right. Then, I'd like to have the "Sakura Course."

R: Very well, sir. For the main dish, would you like the abalone or fillet steak?

G: Well, let me think. . . . Okay, I ¹⁸· _____ a fillet steak.

R: Certainly, sir. After the main dish, ¹⁹· _____ desserts will be brought for you to choose from. ²⁰· _____ to have a cup of coffee, tea, or something else with dessert?

G: Sure. I would like to have a cup of cappuccino if possible.

R: Certainly, sir.

After Listening

Writing & Presentation

ペアを作り、レストラン・スタッフが食事に来たゲストからの苦情や要望に対応する会話を作ってみましょう。苦情や要望の内容、程度、背景を自由に変更して考えてみましょう。適切で迅速に対応するとともに、ゲストの気持ちを汲んだ英語表現を使うなど、ゲストが満足するように工夫しましょう。そして、グループ同士で、あるいはクラス全体でプレゼンテーションしてみましょう。

Additional Listening & Comprehension Questions

2人の会話を聞き、内容に関する質問の答えとして最も適切な選択肢を選びましょう。

🎧 DL 60, 61　💿 CD 60　💿 CD 61

1. Why did the guest have to wait before ordering at the restaurant?
    a. Because the restaurant was very crowded.
    b. Because the restaurant was not open.
    c. Because the guest ordered a cup of coffee first.
    d. Because the guest had no appetite.

2. Who did the guest go to the restaurant with?
    a. His son　b. His daughter　c. His wife　d. His friend

3. Why did the guest feel bad at the restaurant?
    a. Because another guest got his lunch sooner than he did.
    b. Because another guest got his lunch later than he did.
    c. Because the lunch was not satisfactory in quality.
    d. Because the lunch was not satisfactory in quantity.

4. Who will the guest talk with on the phone in the end?
    a. The operator　　　b. The manager
    c. Another guest　　　d. Another front desk clerk

Useful Tips for Providing Hotel Services

恐るべし目のコミュニケーション

苦情対応では、本テキストのスキットで学習したお詫びの単語や表現も重要ですが、人と人との間には、国や文化、言語の違いを超えて、言葉よりもどんな風に言うかや、非言語行動でどのように対応するのかが重要です。謝罪する場合は、相手の目をしっかり見て、気持ちを込めて誠実に、謝罪しなければなりません。日本では、昔から「目は口ほどに物を言う」と言いますが、目つきだけでゲストを怒らせ苦情に発展することもあります。それは、ゲストに対するネガティブな気持ちが目から伝わってしまったからに他なりません。逆に、英語が上手く話せなくても、明るく優しいまなざしや態度でホスピタリティーを表現することも可能です。重要なことは、ゲストに対して常に歓迎の気持ちを忘れずにいることです。

Unit 13

Taking Care of a Guest's Illness
Handling a Complaint:
No Callback from the Banquet Manager

ゲストが病気になったら？／苦情対応―宴会マネジャーから電話が来ない

 Pre-Listening

Key Vocabulary

次の定義に当てはまる語句を、選択肢から選びましょう。

[   ] 1. a bad cold with high fever
[   ] 2. a desire for food
[   ] 3. a doctor who stays in a company or a hotel to give medical care to its employees or guests
[   ] 4. an arranged meeting with someone at a particular time and place
[   ] 5. an outward sign of a disease
[   ] 6. money in coins or bills
[   ] 7. to give an impression of being something
[   ] 8. to give one thing and receive another in return
[   ] 9. to meet someone to give a medical examination
[   ] 10. very bad

| **a.** appetite | **b.** appointment | **c.** cash | **d.** exchange | **e.** flu |
| **f.** house doctor | **g.** see | **h.** seem | **i.** symptom | **j.** terrible |

Understanding Basic Expressions

次の基本表現の音声を聞き、どこに強勢（アクセント）を置くか確認しましょう。音声をまねて繰り返し音読し、同時に意味を考えてみましょう。

1. His clinic is about a 10-minute taxi ride from this hotel.
2. Shall I make an appointment with the doctor for you?
3. What seems to be the problem?
4. Shall I tell the doctor's office about your symptoms?
5. How long have you had these symptoms?
6. Be sure to take some cash in Japanese yen with you.
7. They don't accept credit cards.
8. You can exchange your traveler's checks at the Front Desk.
9. If you need more help, please let us know.
10. I hope you'll feel better soon.

心を伝えるおもてなし表現

I'm afraid not.「あいにく、ホテルに医師はいません」
この表現は "Do you have a house doctor in this hotel?" の返事として使用されています。文法的には、"No, we don't." と言っても問題ないですが、ゲストの期待に沿えないことを申し訳なく思う気持ちを表現して "I'm afraid not." と返事をし、大変丁寧な応対となっています。

Shall I make an appointment with the doctor for you?
「その医師に予約を取りましょうか？」
体調が悪いと訴えるゲストのニーズを先回りして、病院の予約を取ろうと提案しています。さらに for you を最後につけることで、「あなたのために」行うことを表現しています。

Oh, that's too bad.「それは大変ですね」
相手が体調の悪さを訴えた時などに、その辛さに思いを寄せて言う表現です。"That's terrible." も同様の意味です。

If you need more help, please let us know.
「もし、さらにお手伝いできることがございましたら、お知らせください」
困った状況にいるゲストに対して、この表現で温かい気持ちを伝えることができます。

I hope you'll feel better soon.「どうか早くお元気になりますように」
feel better は「気分が良くなる」という意味です。相手の回復を願う優しい表現ですので、体調の悪い人には積極的に用いましょう。

While Listening

Comprehension Questions 🎧 DL 63, 64   ◎ CD 63   ◎ CD 64

A 2人の会話を聞き、内容の順に選択肢を並べ替えましょう。

1.____ → 2.____ → 3.____ → 4.____ → 5.____ → 6.____ → 7.____ → 8.____

a. The concierge advises the guest to take some cash in Japanese yen with him.
b. The concierge asks the guest his age.
c. The concierge gives the guest a map to the clinic.
d. The concierge makes a phone call to the doctor.
e. The concierge offers to make a doctor's appointment for the guest.
f. The guest gives the concierge his name and room number.
g. The guest says that he has something wrong with his physical condition.
h. The guest tells the concierge his symptoms.

B 会話の内容に関する質問の答えとして、最も適切な選択肢を選びましょう。

1. How is the guest feeling now?
   a. Good   b. Angry   c. Bad   d. Hungry

2. Where is the English speaking doctor?
   a. In the hotel   b. In a taxi
   c. At a clinic   d. In a hospital near the airport

3. When did the guest's symptoms start?
   a. The previous night   b. The previous afternoon
   c. That morning   d. That afternoon

4. Who is Mr. Brown?
   a. A concierge   b. A hotel guest
   c. A house doctor   d. An English-speaking doctor

5. What is the map for?
   a. To show the doctor the way to the hotel
   b. To show the guest the way to the hotel
   c. To show the concierge the way to the clinic
   d. To show the taxi driver the way to the clinic

6. What does the clinic accept?

   a. Traveler's checks   **b.** American dollars

   c. Japanese yen   **d.** Credit cards

Dictation Exercise

会話をもう一度聞き、空所に語句を書き入れましょう。

 DL 63   CD 63

Concierge: Good afternoon, sir. How may I help you?

Guest: I feel sick. Do you have ¹_____ in this hotel?

C: I'm ²_____. But we can ³_____ an English speaking doctor near here. His clinic is about a 10-minute taxi ride from this hotel. Shall I make ⁴_____ the doctor for you?

G: Yes. please.

C: Certainly, sir. What ⁵_____ to be the problem?

G: I ⁶_____. I think I have a cold or the flu.

C: Oh, ⁷_____. ⁸_____ tell the doctor's office about your symptoms?

G: Yes, I have a headache, sore throat, and no appetite. I think I feel feverish.

C: How long ⁹_____ these symptoms?

G: Since last night.

C: ¹⁰_____. May I have your name and room number, please?

G: Sure. My name is Thomas Brown, room 1010.

C: And may I tell the doctor's office your age?

G: Sure, I'm 50 years old.

C: I'll call the doctor's clinic and make an appointment for you. Would you wait ¹¹_____?

 DL 64   CD 64

After a phone call to the clinic.

Concierge: Mr. Brown, I called the English speaking doctor's clinic and explained your symptoms. They say the doctor can ¹²_____ now.

Guest: That's good. Thank you.

C: ⁱ³._____. The clinic's name is Tokyo Clinic. ¹⁴._____ a map to the clinic. You can show this to the taxi driver. And ¹⁵._____ take some cash in Japanese yen with you since they don't ¹⁶._____ credit cards.

G: Oh, I don't have much cash in Japanese yen, but I have some traveler's checks in American dollars.

C: You can exchange your traveler's checks at the Front Desk ¹⁷._____. Oh, please ¹⁸._____.

G: I see. Thank you very much for your help.

C: You're quite welcome. If you ¹⁹._____, please ²⁰._____. I hope you'll feel better soon.

After Listening

Writing & Presentation

ペアを作り、気分の優れないゲストにコンシェルジュが病院を紹介する会話を作ってみましょう。まず、ゲストから症状を聞き取って、英語の話せる医師がいる適切な病院を紹介し、アクセス方法や支払方法に関する注意事項をゲストに説明してみましょう。この流れをふまえつつ内容は自由に変更して考えてみましょう。コンシェルジュは体調が悪いゲストに思いやりのある言葉遣いをし、ゲストが安心できるような対応に努めましょう。そして、グループ同士で、あるいはクラス全体でプレゼンテーションしてみましょう。

Additional Listening & Comprehension Questions

2人の会話を聞き、内容に関する質問の答えとして最も適切な選択肢を選びましょう。

DL 65, 66　　CD 65　　CD 66

1. Who calls the Front Desk?
   a. A banquet server　b. A guest　c. A reservationist　d. A manager

2. What does the guest talk about with the front desk clerk?
   a. The menu for the banquet
   b. The cost of the banquet
   c. The importance of the banquet
   d. The number of the guests at the banquet

3. What is the purpose of the banquet?
   a. To solve a problem
   b. To cook delicious food
   c. To invite important customers
   d. To train the employees

4. What kind of request did the guest make in the morning?
   a. To have the banquet manager contact the front desk clerk
   b. To have the front desk clerk contact the guest
   c. To have the banquet manager contact the guest
   d. To have the banquet manager give the guest a refund

Useful Tips for Providing Hotel Services

ホテル全体で病気のゲストに対応

人が助けを最も必要と感じるのは、体調を崩した時ではないでしょうか？ そんな時、そばにいる接客担当者が何とかお手伝いをしたいものです。大きな都市を中心として英語で対応する病院やクリニックは増えてきましたが、近隣にあるそのような施設を事前に調べて最新情報をデータ化しておきましょう。代表的な病気の名前、症状などの英語表現を学習しておく必要もあります。一流といわれるホテルでは、ゲストが病気になったら顧客情報として記録し、それをホテル全体で共有することにより、チェック・アウトまで何かあれば適切にフォロー・アップしていきます。このような病気のゲストに声をかける場合は、Unit 10 の「心を伝えるおもてなし表現」で解説したように、"How are you feeling?"「ご気分はいかがでしょうか？」です。顧客情報の活用により、どこの部署のスタッフもこの表現でゲストの体調を気遣うことができれば、ゲストは安心され喜ばれることでしょう。それが最高の「おもてなし」の一つなのです。

著者紹介

岩井千春
大阪外国語大学外国語学部英語学科を卒業後、株式会社ロイヤルホテルに勤務。
ニューヨークでのグループホテル勤務を経て、本社の人事部で採用・教育を担当。
英語教育の責任者及び接遇サービス研修の講師等を務める。
退職後、大阪大学大学院言語文化研究科博士前期・後期課程を修了。言語文化学博士。
現在、大阪府立大学高等教育推進機構教授。専門分野は英語教育学、観光学であり、
観光業における英語での接遇を研究している。
主要著書は『ESP教育のニーズ分析―産学のグローバル人材育成を目指して』(大阪公立大学共同出版会)。

増崎恒
広島大学文学部文学科英語学英文学専攻を卒業後、広島大学大学院文学研究科博士
前期・後期課程を修了。博士(文学)。
現在、追手門学院大学国際教養学部英語コミュニケーション学科准教授。
専門分野はアメリカ文学。主な研究業績としては、『アメリカスのまなざし―再魔術
化される観光―』(共著)、『アメリカ文学における階級―格差社会の本質を問う』(共著)、『アメリカス世界のなかの「帝国」』(共著) がある。

野澤和典
宇都宮大学教育学部卒業後、カンザス大学大学院修士課程(米国)へ留学し、M.A.
(TESL)取得。
名古屋外国語専門学校講師、豊橋技術科学大学助手・講師・助教授を経て、現在立
命館大学情報理工学部及び大学院言語教育情報研究科教授。
専門分野は応用言語学。『最新ICTを活用した私の外国語授業』(共編著)ほか著書
論文多数。Apple Distinguished Educator 2013. CALL-EJ 共編者。

**Hospitality English
for Careers at Hotels**

おもてなしのホテル英語

2015年2月20日　初版第1刷発行
2024年10月15日　初版第4刷発行

著者　岩　井　千　春
　　　増　崎　　　恒
　　　野　崎　和　典

発行者　福　岡　正　人
発行所　株式会社　金星堂
（〒101-0051）東京都千代田区神田神保町 3-21
Tel.（03）3263-3828（営業部）
（03）3263-3997（編集部）
Fax（03）3263-0716
https://www.kinsei-do.co.jp

編集担当／西田碧、長島吉成　　　　　Printed in Japan
印刷所・製本所／倉敷印刷株式会社
本書の無断複製・複写は著作権法上での例外を除き禁じられています。
本書を代行業者等の第三者に依頼してスキャンやデジタル化することは、
たとえ個人や家庭内での利用であっても認められておりません。
落丁・乱丁本はお取り替えいたします。

ISBN978-4-7647-1142-6　　C1082